ZAGAT®

Hawaii Restaurants

LOCAL EDITOR
Jeanette Foster

STAFF EDITOR
Yoji Yamaguchi

Published and distributed by
Zagat Survey, LLC
4 Columbus Circle
New York, NY 10019
T: 212.977.6000
E: hawaii@zagat.com
www.zagat.com

ACKNOWLEDGMENTS

We thank Diane Ako, Candy Aluli, Laura Aquino, Ruth Ann Becker, Yvonne Biegel, Patricia Blackburn, Kelii Brown, Nancy Brown, Nancy Daniels, Jessica Ferracane, Marylou Foley, Bonnie Friedman, Rick Gaffney, Diann Hartman, Donna Jung, Charlene Kauhane, Margaret Kearns, Vicki Kometani, Candice Kraughto, Waynette Kwon, Priscilla Life, Joan Matsumoto, Liana Mulleitner, Brad Packer, Rebecca Pang, Cynthia Rankin, Stephanie Kaluahine Reid, Mari Takamura, Jeanette Vidgen, Donna Wheeler, Donna Marino Wilkins, Caroline Witherspoon, Aven Wright-McIntosh and Sandi Yara, as well as the following members of our staff: Josh Rogers (senior associate editor), Brian Albert, Sean Beachell, Maryanne Bertollo, Sandy Cheng, Reni Chin, Larry Cohn, Nicole Diaz, Alison Flick, Jeff Freier, Matthew Hamm, Marc Henson, Natalie Lebert, Mike Liao, Polina Paley, Art Yaghci, Sharon Yates, Anna Zappia and Kyle Zolner.

ISBN-13: 978-1-60478-432-9
ISBN-10: 1-60478-432-6
Printed in the
United States of America

Contents

Ratings & Symbols 4
About This Survey 5
What's New 6
Glossary 7
Map 8
Top Statewide Ratings 9

RESTAURANT DIRECTORY

Names, Locations, Contact Info, Ratings and Reviews
Oahu 14
Maui 57
Big Island 78
Kauai 90
Lanai & Molokai 100

INDEXES

Cuisines 104
Locations 111
Special Features 118

Ratings & Symbols

Zagat Top Spot	Name	Symbols	Cuisine	Zagat Ratings: FOOD	DECOR	SERVICE	COST
Z	Tim & Nina's	◐	*Hawaiian*	▽ 18	13	20	$15

Area, Address & Contact
Waikiki | 1 Tiki Place (Kalakaua Ave.) | 808-977-6000 | www.zagat.com

Review, surveyor comments in quotes
The staff shows "plenty of aloha spirit" at this "local Hawaiian favorite" in Waikiki where the "umbrella-ed mai tais are strong", the pupus "plentiful" and the Diamond Head views "dazzling"; kamaaina are less crazy about the "tiki-tacky" decor with "enough torches and conch shells to start your own luau", but at least the price is right.

Ratings **Food, Decor** & **Service** are rated on a 30 pt. scale.

0 - 9	poor to fair
10 - 15	fair to good
16 - 19	good to very good
20 - 25	very good to excellent
26 - 30	extraordinary to perfection
▽	low response | less reliable

Cost The estimated price of a dinner with one drink and tip. Lunch is usually 25% less. For unrated **newcomers** or **write-ins,** the price range is shown as follows:

I	$25 and below	E	$41 to $65
M	$26 to $40	VE	$66 or above

Symbols

Z	highest ratings, popularity and importance
◐	serves after 11 PM
S M	closed on Sunday or Monday
≠	no credit cards accepted

About This Survey

Here are the results of our latest **Hawaii Restaurants Survey,** covering 389 eateries (with additional listings online). Like all our guides, this one is based on input from avid local consumers - 2,942 all told.

THREE SIMPLE PREMISES underlie our ratings and reviews. First, we believe that the collective opinions of large numbers of consumers are more accurate than those of any single person. (Consider that our surveyors bring some 474,000 annual meals' worth of experience to this year's survey.) Second, food quality is only part of the equation when choosing a restaurant, thus we ask surveyors to separately rate food, decor and service and report on cost. Third, since people need reliable information in a fast, easy-to-digest format, we strive to be concise and we offer our content on every platform - print, online and mobile.

ABOUT ZAGAT: In 1979, we started asking friends to rate and review restaurants purely for fun. That hobby grew into Zagat Survey; 32 years later, we have over 375,000 surveyors and cover everything from airlines to shopping in over 100 countries. Along the way, we evolved from being a print publisher to a digital content provider, e.g. **ZAGAT.com, ZAGAT.mobi** (for web-enabled mobile devices), **ZAGAT TO GO** (for smartphones) and **nru** (for Android phones). We also produce customized gifts and marketing tools for a wide range of corporate clients. And you can find us on Twitter (twitter.com/zagat), Facebook and just about any other social media network.

THANKS: We're especially grateful to our local editor, Jeanette Foster, who has edited our Hawaii Surveys since 1997.

JOIN IN: To improve our guides, we solicit your comments. Just contact us at **nina-tim@zagat.com.** We also invite you to join our surveys at **ZAGAT.com.** If you do, you'll receive a choice of rewards in exchange.

New York, NY
April 6, 2011

Nina and Tim Zagat

What's New

SURF'S UP: Prices have been on the rise in paradise but dining out remains a way of life for many in Hawaii. Our surveyors report eating out an average of 3.1 times per week (down just slightly from 3.2 in our last survey), and foodies are flocking to new high-end restaurants across the island chain.

BIG KAHUNAS: Hawaii has its share of notables (see under: 44th President), and surveyors are happy to see even more of them in the kitchen, with 43% giving a thumbs-up to the toques-turned-celeb trend. Big-name chefs landing in Waikiki include "Iron Chef" Masaharu Morimoto, whose **Morimoto Waikiki** is dishing out his signature Japanese fare in the new Waikiki Edition Hotel, and Laurent Tourondel, who opened **BLT Steak** in the Trump International. On Kauai, Jean-Georges Vongerichten's **Kauai Grill** in the St. Regis Princeville is offering Eclectic fare plus incredible views of Hanalei Bay.

NA MEA 'AI O NA 'AINA: Whether it's the daily catch from local fishing fleets, grass-fed beef from Wailea or Hamakua mushrooms, Hawaii's bounty stars on the menus of many top chefs, no doubt pleasing the 74% of surveyors who think it's important that food be "green" (i.e. locally sourced, organic or sustainably raised). At her latest venture, **Gannon's - A Pacific View Restaurant,** Beverly Gannon (**Hali'imaile General Store, Joe's**) serves her popular Hawaii Regional cuisine at a Wailea location with (you guessed it) a Pacific view. Peter Merriman has opened a seafood-centric branch of his eponymous Hawaii Regional in Koloa's Kukui'ula Village shopping center on Kauai, serving local day-boat catches and raw bar selections, while D.K. Kodama (of **Sansei, Vino** and **DK** fame) offers an all-day menu of Hawaiian farm-to-table fare at his **Cane & Taro** in Maui's Kaanapali's Whaler's Village.

SURVEY STATS: The average meal cost reported by Hawaii surveyors is $37.66, while the average tip is 18.7% (vs. the national average of 19.2%) . . . Service is the top dining-out irritant, cited by 57% of surveyors, with noise a distant second (14%) . . . Only 10% reserve online, but that's more than double the 4% who did so in our last survey.

Kailua-Kona, HI
April 6, 2011

Jeanette Foster

Glossary

The following is a brief glossary of Hawaiian terms.

Ahi: yellowfin tuna
Grinds: food
Hapuupuu: sea bass
Humuhumunukunukuapua'a (aka Humu Humu): reef trigger fish; state fish of Hawaii
Imu: underground oven
Kalua pork: pork cooked in an underground oven
Kamaaina: longtime resident of Hawaii
Kau kau: food
Keiki: children
Kiawe-grilled: grilled over aromatic wood
Lanai: terrace or patio
Laulau: pork, beef or fish steamed in ti leaves
Lilikoi: passion fruit
Loco Moco: a heap of white rice topped with a hamburger and a fried egg, smothered in gravy
Luau: Hawaiian feast
Lumpia: Philippine egg roll
Mahalo: thanks, gratitude; to thank
Makai: in the direction of the sea
Malihini: newcomer, tourist
Mauka: toward the mountains, upland
Ohana: family
Ono: delicious
Paniolo: Hawaiian cowboy
Plate lunch: two scoops of rice and macaroni salad served with fried fish, beef or chicken
Poi: taro pounded in a liquid form
Poke: cubed raw fish with onions and seaweed
Pupu: appetizer
Saimin: a thin broth with noodles, vegetables and fish, chicken or pork
Shave ice: snow cone
Taro: edible, starchy root, similar to potato
Ti: leaf used in cooking, serving and decorating
Wikiwiki: quick

MOST POPULAR - BY ISLAND

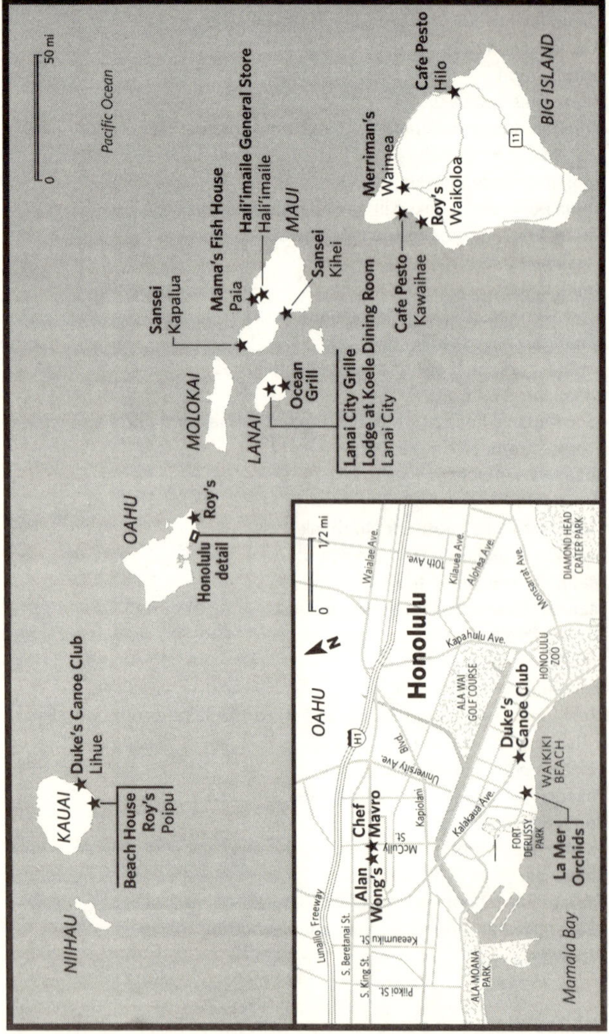

Most Popular - By Island

OAHU

1. Alan Wong's | *Hawaii Reg.*
2. Roy's | *Hawaii Reg.*
3. La Mer | *French*
4. Chef Mavro | *Fr./Hawaii Reg.*
5. Duke's Canoe Club | *American*
6. Orchids | *Pacific Rim*

MAUI

1. Mama's Fish House | *Seafood*
2. Hali'imaile General | *Hawaii Reg.*
3. Sansei | *Japanese/Pac. Rim*

BIG ISLAND

1. Merriman's | *Hawaii Reg.*
2. Roy's | *Hawaii Reg.*
3. Café Pesto | *Eclectic*

KAUAI

1. Beach House | *Pacific Rim*
2. Roy's | *Hawaii Reg.*
3. Duke's Canoe Club | *American*

LANAI

1. Lodge/Koele Din. Rm. | *Pac. Rim*
2. Lanai City Grille | *Pacific Rim*
3. Ocean Grill | *Asian/Seafood*

Most Popular - Statewide

1. Roy's | *multi.*
2. Alan Wong's | *Oahu*
3. Mama's Fish House | *Maui*
4. Merriman's | *multi.*
5. Sansei | *multi.*
6. Hali'imaile General | *Maui*
7. Duke's Canoe Club | *multi.*
8. Beach House | *Kauai*
9. La Mer | *Oahu*
10. Chef Mavro | *Oahu*
11. Ruth's Chris | *multi.*
12. Hula Grill/Hula Grill | *multi.*
13. Lahaina Grill | *Maui*
14. Spago | *Maui*
15. Orchids | *Oahu*
16. David Paul's | *Maui*
17. Pacific'O | *Maui*
18. Cheeseburger/Paradise | *multi.*
19. 3660 on the Rise | *Oahu*
20. Nobu Waikiki | *Oahu*
21. Michel's | *Oahu*
22. Longhi's | *multi.*
23. Hy's Steak House | *Oahu*
24. Plantation House | *Maui*
25. Mala | *Maui*
26. Assaggio | *Oahu*
27. Café Pesto | *Big Island*
28. CanoeHouse | *Big Island*
29. Brown's Beach Hse. | *Big Island*
30. Nick's Fishmarket | *Maui*

Top Food - Statewide

28 Sushi Sasabune | *Oahu*
Hiroshi Eurasion | *Oahu*
Alan Wong's | *Oahu*
La Mer | *Oahu*

27 Mama's Fish | *Maui*
Chef Mavro | *Oahu*
Hali'imaile General | *Maui*
Le Bistro | *Oahu*
Michel's | *Oahu*
Nobu Waikiki | *Oahu*
Lodge/Koele Din. Rm. | *Lanai*

26 Spago | *Maui*
Orchids | *Oahu*
Hakone | *Oahu*
Gerard's | *Maui*
Pahu i'a | *Big Island*
Hy's Steak | *Oahu*
Kauai Grill | *Kauai*
Merriman's | *multi.*
Hilo Bay Café | *Big Island*
Lahaina Grill | *Maui*
David Paul's Island Grill | *Maui*
Hoku's | *Oahu*
Roy's | *multi.*
Ocean Grill | *Lanai*
Paia Fish Market | *Maui*
Red Salt* | *Kauai*

25 Sansei | *multi.*
Ruth's Chris | *multi.*
Flatbread Co. | *Maui*
Capische? | *Maui*
Nico's at Pier 38 | *Oahu*
Helena's Hawaiian | *Oahu*
Kihei Caffe | *Maui*
Bar Acuda | *Kauai*
3660 on the Rise | *Oahu*
Azure | *Oahu*
Dondero's* | *Kauai*
Olive Tree* | *Oahu*
Ono Hawaiian | *Oahu*
Yohei Sushi | *Oahu*
Taormina | *Oahu*
Manta/Pavilion | *Big Island*
Waterfront Rest.* | *Maui*
Pineapple Grill | *Maui*
Sarento's/Beach | *Maui*
Pacific'O | *Maui*
Baci Bistro | *Oahu*
Duo | *Maui*
Mala* | *Maui*

Excludes places with low votes; * indicates a tie with restaurant above

BY CUISINE

AMERICAN

26 Lahaina Grill | *Maui*
25 Kihei Caffe | *Maui*
24 Tangö Cafe | *Oahu*
Gazebo | *Maui*
Town | *Oahu*

CHINESE

23 Little Vill. Noodle Hse. | *Oahu*
Kirin | *Oahu*
22 Pah Ke's | *Oahu*
Fook Yuen | *Oahu*
Ciao Mein | *Oahu*

ECLECTIC

26 Kauai Grill | *Kauai*
24 Banyan Tree | *Maui*
Jackie Rey's | *Big Island*
Keei Café | *Big Island*
CanoeHouse | *Big Island*

FRENCH

28 La Mer | *Oahu*
27 Chef Mavro | *Oahu*
Le Bistro | *Oahu*
Michel's | *Oahu*
26 Gerard's | *Maui*

HAWAIIAN

26 David Paul's Island Grill | *Maui*
Red Salt | *Kauai*
25 Helena's Hawaiian | *Oahu*
Ono Hawaiian | *Oahu*
24 Koloa Fish Market | *Kauai*

HAWAII REGIONAL

28 Alan Wong's | *Oahu*
27 Chef Mavro | *Oahu*
Hali'imaile General | *Maui*
26 Pahu i'a | *Big Island*
Merriman's | *multi.*

ITALIAN

25 Capische? | *Maui*
Dondero's | *Kauai*
Taormina | *Oahu*
Baci Bistro | *Oahu*
24 Arancino | *Oahu*

JAPANESE

28 Sushi Sasabune | *Oahu*
27 Nobu Waikiki | *Oahu*
26 Hakone | *Oahu*
25 Sansei | *multi.*
Yohei Sushi | *Oahu*

MEDITERRANEAN

25 Bar Acuda | *Kauai*
Sarento's/Beach | *Maui*
Plantation House | *Maui*
21 Formaggio | *Oahu*
Merriman's Mkt. | *Big Island*

PACIFIC RIM

27 Mama's Fish | *Maui*
Lodge/Koele Din. Rm. | *Lanai*
26 Spago | *Maui*
Orchids | *Oahu*
Hilo Bay Café | *Big Island*

SEAFOOD

27 Mama's Fish | *Maui*
25 Nico's at Pier 38 | *Oahu*
Azure | *Oahu*
Waterfront Rest. | *Maui*
24 Brown's Beach Hse. | *Big Island*

STEAKHOUSES

26 Hy's Steak | *Oahu*
25 Ruth's Chris | *multi.*
Duo | *Maui*
24 Son'z/Swan Court | *Maui*
Cafe O'Lei | *Maui*

TOP DECOR - STATEWIDE

29 La Mer | *Oahu*
Lodge/Koele Din. Rm. | *Lanai*

28 Orchids | *Oahu*
Pahu i'a | *Big Island*
Kauai Grill | *Kauai*

27 Tidepools | *Kauai*
Michel's | *Oahu*
CanoeHouse | *Big Island*
Spago | *Maui*
Brown's Beach Hse. | *Big Island*
Beachhouse/Moana | *Oahu*
Hau Tree | *Oahu*
Manta & Pavilion | *Big Island*
Son'z/Swan Court | *Maui*
Hoku's | *Oahu*
Mama's Fish | *Maui*
Feast at Lele | *Maui*

26 Humuhumunukunukuapua'a | *Maui*
Ocean Grill | *Lanai*
Beach House | *Kauai*

TOP SERVICE - STATEWIDE

28 La Mer | *Oahu*
Chef Mavro | *Oahu*
Lodge/Koele Din. Rm. | *Lanai*

27 Michel's | *Oahu*
Orchids | *Oahu*
Hy's Steak | *Oahu*
Hiroshi Eurasion | *Oahu*

26 Hoku's | *Oahu*
Hakone | *Oahu*
Gerard's | *Maui*
Alan Wong's | *Oahu*
Pahu i'a | *Big Island*
Spago | *Maui*
Bali Steaks/Seafood | *Oahu*
Son'z/Swan Court | *Maui*

25 Lahaina Grill | *Maui*
Kauai Grill | *Kauai*
Banyan Tree | *Maui*
Dondero's | *Kauai*
Mama's Fish | *Maui*

BEST BUYS - STATEWIDE

1. Matsumoto's Shave Ice | *Oahu*
2. Cafe 100 | *Big Island*
3. Mix Café | *Oahu*
4. Duane's Ono-Char | *Kauai*
5. Goma Tei Ramen | *Oahu*
6. Kua 'Aina Sandwich | *Oahu*
7. Ezogiku | *Oahu*
8. Bubba Burgers | *Kauai*
9. Aloha Mixed Plate | *Maui*
10. Nico's at Pier 38 | *Oahu*
11. Gazebo | *Maui*
12. Tanioka's | *Oahu*
13. Cilantro Grill | *Maui*
14. Maui Tacos | *multi.*
15. Koloa Fish Market | *Kauai*
16. Contemporary Café | *Oahu*
17. Island Burgers | *Oahu*
18. Kozo Sushi | *Oahu*
19. Shirokiya | *Oahu*
20. Highway Inn | *Oahu*

RESTAURANT DIRECTORY

FOOD | DECOR | SERVICE | COST

Oahu

TOP FOOD

- 28 Sushi Sasabune | *Japanese*
- Hiroshi Eurasion | *Eurasian*
- Alan Wong's | *Hawaii Reg.*
- La Mer | *French*
- 27 Chef Mavro | *Fr./Hawaii Reg.*

TOP DECOR

- 29 La Mer
- 28 Orchids
- 27 Michel's
- Beachhouse/Moana
- Hau Tree

TOP SERVICE

- 28 La Mer
- Chef Mavro
- 27 Michel's
- Orchids
- Hy's Steak

BEST BUYS

1. Matsumoto's Shave Ice
2. Mix Café
3. Goma Tei Ramen
4. Kua 'Aina Sandwich
5. Ezogiku

Akasaka ◐ *Japanese* — 24 | 14 | 21 | $40

Ala Moana | 1646 Kona St. (bet. Atkinson Dr. & Kaheka St.) | Honolulu | 808-942-4466

Fans swear that sushi "doesn't get fresher or tastier" than the raw stuff at this "user-friendly" Ala Moana "institution" offering "fantastic", "affordable" Japanese fare and "service with big smiles" in a "high-energy" setting; you're "greeted with a shout" as you enter digs that are "not fancy but pleasant", and while a few fret at the nearby "girlie bars" ("not where you'd want to take the kids"), for many it's an "oasis" that "delivers every time."

Z Alan Wong's *Hawaii Reg.* — 28 | 22 | 26 | $68

McCully | 1857 S. King St. (bet. Hauoli & Pumehana Sts.) | Honolulu | 808-949-2526 | www.alanwongs.com

The place where "Hawaii Regional cuisine was born and still reigns", Alan Wong's longtime standout garners Oahu's No. 1 Most Popular honors thanks to "inspired" cuisine, an "exceptional" wine list and "gracious" service that make it a "must when in Honolulu" for many, including "President Obama"; you can "see the chefs work their magic" in the open kitchen, and though some find the space otherwise "pedestrian" and the location "hard to find", most agree the "heavenly experience" is "well worth the effort" and "pricey" tabs.

Antonio's New York Pizzeria *Pizza* 19 | 7 | 13 | $18

Pearl City | 719 Kamehameha Hwy. (Puu Poni St.) | 808-454-1233 M
Kahala | 4210 Waialae Ave. (Hunakai St.) | Honolulu | 808-737-3333
www.antoniosnypizza.com

Families "on a budget" are fond of this pizzeria pair in Kahala and Pearl City for its "darn good" thin-crust pizzas and "excellent prices"; purists pooh-pooh the pies as "kinda NY, but not really", while others carp about "crabby" service and "dingy" digs, but defenders insist it's one of the "best take-out" options around.

Arancino *Italian* 24 | 19 | 22 | $33

Waikiki | 255 Beachwalk (Kalakaua Ave.) | Honolulu | 808-923-5557

Arancino di Mare *Italian*

Waikiki | Waikiki Beach Marriott Resort & Spa | 2552 Kalakaua Ave. (bet. Ohua & Paoakalani Aves.) | Honolulu | 808-931-6273
www.arancino.net

Many are "pleasantly surprised" by the "wide range of dishes" at this "reliable" Italian duo in Waikiki, including "excellent seafood pastas" such as the spaghetti with uni (sea urchin), while others are taken aback by the "lines of tourists standing outside"; the Marriott branch located "right off the beach" is a "great place to unwind and chill", but some critics find the spaces "small" and complain of "too many tables per server", resulting in "slow" service.

Assaggio *Italian* 21 | 20 | 21 | $33

Kailua | 354 Uluniu St. (bet. Maluniu Ave. & Oneawa St.) | 808-261-2772
Kapolei | 777 Kamokila Blvd. (Uluohia St.) | 808-674-8801
Mililani | Town Center Of Mililani | 95-1249 Meheula Pkwy. (bet. Lanikuhana Ave. & Makaimoimo St.) | 808-623-5115
Ala Moana | Ala Moana Ctr. | 1450 Ala Moana Blvd. (bet. Atkinson Dr. & Piikoi St.) | Honolulu | 808-942-3446
Hawaii Kai | Koko Marina Ctr. | 7192 Kalanianaole Hwy. (Lunalilo Home Rd.) | Honolulu | 808-396-0756
NEW **Kahala** | 4346 Waialae Ave. (Kalanianaole Hwy.) | Honolulu | 808-732-1011
www.assaggiohi.com

Fans attest you "get your money's worth" at this "well-established", "reliable" Italian chain offering a "large menu" of "consistently good" "red-sauce" fare at "reasonable prices" (the tableside Caesar salad is "always a treat") and "friendly, Hawaiian-style service" in a "pleasant", "classy "setting; the "decor is simple, but in good taste", and the Hawaii Kai branch offers "nice views" of Koko Marina.

Auntie Pasto's *Italian* 19 | 14 | 18 | $24

Waipahu | Kunia Shopping Ctr. | 94-673 Kupuohi St. (Kapuna Loop) | 808-680-0005

Downtown | 1099 S. Beretania St. (Pensacola St.) | Honolulu | 808-523-8855

www.auntiepastos.com

These Italian twins in Downtown Honolulu and Waipahu are "go-to restaurants" for a "younger crowd" as well as "big families with big appetites", dishing out "robust", "basic" eats at "reasonable" prices amid "homey" surroundings; they're "always crowded and busy", but the staff remains "friendly and accommodating", and while some detractors dismiss them as "nothing special", fans insist they're a "great value."

Azure *Seafood* 25 | 25 | 22 | $66

Waikiki | Royal Hawaiian Hotel | 2259 Kalakaua Ave. (Royal Hawaiian Ave.) | Honolulu | 808-923-7311 | www.azurewaikiki.com

"Prepare to have your socks knocked off" by the "beautiful setting" on Waikiki Beach and "sophisticated" interior "with a classic design that manages to be hip" at this "upscale" seafooder housed in the Royal Hawaiian Hotel, where "culinary artist" Jon Matsubara's "fresh", "innovative" maritime fare is "at the top of its game" and the service is "excellent"; if a few grumble that the "cost is high", many others conclude the "prices are fair"; P.S. "reserve a cabana on the beach for the ultimate romantic experience."

Baci Bistro *Italian* 25 | 20 | 24 | $38

Kailua | 30 Aulike St. (bet. Kuulei Rd. & Uluniu St.) | 808-262-7555 | www.bacibistro.com

Even though it's "hidden away on the windward side of Oahu", this "delightful" "little Italian bistro" "fills up fast" thanks to a "varied menu" of "superb", "authentic" cuisine served by a "knowledgeable", "dedicated" staff, and a "friendly" owner who "always greets you with a warm welcome"; "nice outdoor seating" is an alternative to the "small" dining room where some find the "tables uncomfortably close together, even in friendly Kailua."

Bac Nam ☒ *Vietnamese* 23 | 10 | 19 | $19

Downtown | 1117 S. King St. (bet. Pensacola & Piikoi Sts.) | Honolulu | 808-597-8201

Phonatics call this "lovely family-run Vietnamese" in Downtown "one of Honolulu's best" for "fresh", "authentic" cuisine, including "excellent sandwiches", "rich, flavorful" pho and "lots of dishes not found anywhere else"; the service is "friendly", if sometimes "a bit slow", and though "small and plain" it may be, most agree the "top-notch" eats and "reasonable" prices make it "worth a drive."

Bali Steaks & Seafood ☒ Ⓜ *Pacific Rim* 24 | 25 | 26 | $57

(fka Bali by the Sea)

Waikiki | Hilton Hawaiian Vill. | 2005 Kalia Rd. (Ala Moana Blvd.) | Honolulu | 808-941-2254 | www.hiltonhawaiianvillage.com

Housed in the Rainbow Tower of the Hilton Hawaiian Village in Waikiki, this "romantic" Pacific Rim spot is the "epitome of class", offering "terrific" service in an "enchanting", "romantic" space with an "old-school atmosphere" and "incredible views" of the beach; throw in some "excellent" cooking, and you'll see why so many "highly recommend it for a date."

Beachhouse at the Moana *American/Steak* 23 | 27 | 22 | $61

Waikiki | Moana Surfrider | 2365 Kalakaua Ave. (Kaiulani Ave.) | Honolulu | 808-921-4600 | www.beachhousewaikiki.com

The "only way to be closer to the ocean is to get on a boat" attest fans of this "pricey" New American steakhouse housed in the "stately", "glamorous" Moana Surfrider resort in Waikiki, where "awesome views from the veranda" add to the "allure and romance" of the experience and the "creatively prepared" fare is served by an "attentive" staff; still, a few spoilers say the "food does not live up to the setting" and report "mechanical" service at times; P.S. "afternoon tea is a delightful alternative" to a full meal.

Benihana *Japanese* 19 | 19 | 21 | $48

Waikiki | Hilton Hawaiian Vill. | 2005 Kalia Rd. (Ala Moana Blvd.) | Honolulu | 808-955-5955 | www.benihana.com

While it may be "typical of the chain", this Waikiki outpost of the teppanyaki behemoth is "more attractive" than most, thanks to its setting in the Hilton Hawaiian Village, where "theatrical" chefs "chop and slice" at tableside grills, providing "great entertainment for kids and adults" while preparing "consistent", "tasty" fare; cynics may knock it as "tacky" and "touristy", but many recommend it for families who want to "enjoy a happy occasion."

Big City Diner *American* 17 | 14 | 19 | $20

Kailua | Foodland Mktpl. | 108 Hekili St. (Hamakua Dr.) | 808-263-8880

Waipahu | Waipio Shopping Ctr. | 94-800 Ukee St. (Oil Loop) | 808-678-8868

Aiea | Pearlridge Ctr. E. | 98-211 Pali Momi St. (Haukapila St.) | 808-487-8188

Kaimuki | 3565 Waialae Ave. (bet. 11th & 12th Aves.) | Honolulu | 808-738-8855

Ward | Ward Entertainment Ctr. | 1060 Auahi St. (bet. Kamakee St. & Ward Ave.) | Honolulu | 808-591-8891

www.bigcitydinerhawaii.com

The "friendly, helpful" staff "always greets you with aloha" at this "dependable" chain dishing out "ample portions" of "stick-to-your-ribs" American comfort food "with a local twist", "for not a lot of cash"; the "casual" setting has an "old-time diner feeling", and while cynics say it's all "about quantity not quality", the "relaxed" vibe and "good value" make it a popular "family favorite."

NEW **BLT Steak** *Steak* 24 | 24 | 22 | $70

Waikiki | Trump International | 223 Saratoga Rd. (Kalia Rd.) | Honolulu | 808-683-7440 | www.bltsteak.com

In a "city without great steakhouses", this Waikiki Trump Hotel outpost of Laurent Tourondel's empire is a "good addition to the local scene", delivering "excellent" steaks and "smooth" service amid "pleasant surroundings" with "elegant lighting" and a "NY" ambiance; still, some are nonplussed by the "very expensive" tabs.

Brasserie Du Vin ◐ Ⓢ *French* 22 | 22 | 20 | $36

Chinatown | 1115 Bethel St. (bet. Hotel & Pauahi Sts.) | Honolulu | 808-545-1115 | www.brasserieduvin.com

"Paris in Chinatown" is how fans describe this "lovely hideaway" boasting a "delightful French courtyard" and an "impressive wooden bar", where the "light" Gallic entrees and small plates are "high-quality", the "carefully selected" wine list "can't be beat" and the happy-hour deals are "incredible"; the staff is "friendly", and if there's "nothing with a 'wow' factor" here, many nonetheless consider this "charming" spot "worth the hassle of finding a place to park."

Bubba Gump Shrimp Co. *American/Seafood* 16 | 18 | 18 | $28

Ala Moana | Ala Moana Ctr. | 1450 Ala Moana Blvd. (bet. Atkinson Dr. & Piikoi St.) | Honolulu | 808-949-4867 | www.bubbagump.com

"Travelers with children" and "fans of the movie" applaud this "family-friendly" and "not too pricey" American chain for its "dependable" seafood, "quick" service and "laid-back" setting full of film "memorabilia"; critics dismiss it as a "tourist trap" with "mediocre eats" and "over-cutesy theme decor", but defenders insist it's a "good value."

Burgers on the Edge *Burgers* 17 | 12 | 16 | $15

Kapahulu | Avenue Shops at Safeway | 890 Kapahulu Ave. (Olu St.) | Honolulu | 808-737-8866 | www.burgersontheedge.com

You "order your ground meat" and choose from a "generous" selection of toppings to "create your own" "over-the-top" hamburger at this Kapahulu eatery, where "there's not much to say" about the "simple" surroundings; fans also "love" the sweet potato and truffle fries, and put it "two notches above other fast-food burger joints", but some dissenters find it "pricey" and "somewhat short of memorable."

Buzz's Lanikai ⌧ *Steak* 20 | 20 | 20 | $35

Lanikai | 413 Kawailoa Rd. (bet. Kawailoa & Popoia Rds.) | Kailua | 808-261-4661

Buzz's Pearl City *Steak*

Pearl City | 98-751 Kuahao Pl. (Kaahumanu St.) | 808-487-6465 www.buzzssteakhouse.com

Set in a "raffish" bungalow with "beachy decor" located "across the road from the beach in Lanikai", this "windward landmark" (and its "stalwart" sibling in Pearl City) is a "red meat lover's delight", while appealing to finatics as well with "fresh local fish"; "killer mai tais" and other "exotic cocktails" add to the buzz, and "friendly service" seals the deal; the Kohala Coast sibling is adjacent to the Beach Golf Course at the Waikoloa Beach Resort.

Cafe Sistina *Italian* 21 | 23 | 20 | $32

Makiki | 1314 S. King St. (bet. Keeaumoku & Piikio Sts.) | Honolulu | 808-596-0061 | www.cafesistina.com

It's almost like dining at the "Vatican" at this Makiki Northern Italian where "impressive", "original" murals "à la Michelangelo" grace the walls, setting the stage for "large portions" of "straightforward" "comfort food" as well as more "exotic" creations; still, some report "inconsistent" quality and service and lament that, save for the "astonishing" artwork, "everything falls just short of being truly memorable."

California Beach Rock 'N Sushi *Japanese* 20 | 14 | 19 | $29

Ward | Ward Ctr. | 404 Ward Ave. (Halekauwila St.) | Honolulu | 808-597-8000 | www.californiabeachrocknsushi.com

The "early-bird special is one of the best deals in town" at this Ward Japanese whose "creative, delicious" sushi makes it a "locals' favorite" for "terrific casual dining"; the "small" digs are "usually crowded" and "loud", but "quick" service gets you in and out efficiently, and while a few purists sniff that it's "not authentic", "reasonable" prices make it a "good value" and ensure that you'll "never leave hungry."

California Pizza Kitchen *Pizza* 20 | 17 | 19 | $24

Kailua | Kailua Town Ctr. | 609 Kailua Rd. (Kuulei Rd.) | 808-263-2480
Aiea | Pearlridge Ctr. | 554 Pearlridge Ctr. (Rose Rd.) | 808-487-7741
Ala Moana | Ala Moana Ctr. | 1450 Ala Moana Blvd. (bet. Atkinson Dr. & Piikoi St.) | Honolulu | 808-941-7715
Waikiki | 2284 Kalakaua Ave. (Seaside Ave.) | Honolulu | 808-924-2000
www.cpk.com

"Clever", "unusual" pizzas and "creative" salads are the "stars" at this "gourmet" pie chain providing "something for everyone's taste"; it's "inexpensive", "prompt" and "consistent", though critics complain the "wannabe eclectic offerings" have grown "tired" and the "overlit" surroundings just "don't have any charm."

Chai's Island Bistro *Pacific Rim* 25 | 22 | 23 | $48

Downtown | Aloha Tower Mktpl. | 1 Aloha Tower Dr. (Ala Moana Blvd.) | Honolulu | 808-585-0011 | www.chaisislandbistro.com

Chef Chai Chaowasaree's "fresh, innovative" Pacific Rim cuisine plus live entertainment from "top-notch Hawaiian musicians" "make for a winning combination" at his "refined" Aloha Tower Marketplace establishment, where the "picturesque", "tropical" setting includes an outdoor dining garden for those who find the room "too noisy"; while a few say they "expected much better, given the prices", for many it's "always a good choice."

Cheeseburger in Paradise *American* 17 | 18 | 17 | $22

Waikiki | 1945 Kalakaua Ave. (Ala Moana Blvd.) | Honolulu | 808-941-2400

Waikiki | 2500 Kalakaua Ave. (Kealohilani St.) | Honolulu | 808-923-3731

www.cheeseburgerland.com

When you're tired of "overpriced seafood" and crave a "classic cheeseburger with a tropical twist", fans recommend these "kitschy, fun" burger chain links that are "not ashamed to be tourist traps", offering "good value for the money", as well as "great entertainment" and "fantastic drinks"; detractors, though, declare the fare "pedestrian", decry the staff for trying to "upsell you on everything" and dismiss its popularity as a "tribute to fine marketing."

Cheesecake Factory *American* 20 | 19 | 19 | $30

Waikiki | Royal Hawaiian Ctr. | 2301 Kalakaua Ave. (Duke's Ln.) | Honolulu | 808-924-5001 | www.thecheesecakefactory.com

"Humongous portions and humongous lines" characterize the Waikiki outpost of this American chain where the "textbook"-size menu offers "lots of choices" and a "broad price spectrum" to keep families "stuffed and happy"; the "herd 'em in, herd 'em out" feel isn't for everyone and critics knock "mass-produced" fare and "overdone" decor, but overall it's a "crowd-pleaser", especially when it comes to the "amazing" namesake dessert - plus it's located "in the middle of all the hotels."

Z Chef Mavro S M *French/Hawaii Reg.* 27 | 25 | 28 | $93

Moiliili | 1969 S. King St. (McCully St.) | Honolulu | 808-944-4714 | www.chefmavro.com

Though it "doesn't look like much from the outside", set on a "busy corner" in Moiliili, George Mavrothalassitis' Hawaii Regional-French standout offers "an evening not to be missed", featuring "perfectly prepared" and "beautifully presented" dishes, "spot-on" wine pairings, "stellar" service and "elegant" decor; you'll pay a "hefty price" (and still "walk out hungry" grouse some), but most agree the "memorable experience" is "worth every penny."

Chiang Mai Thai *Thai* 20 | 18 | 18 | $26

Moiliili | 2239 S. King St. (Makahiki Way) | Honolulu | 808-941-1151 | www.808chiangmai.com

There's "no drama" at this Moiliili Thai, just a "comfortable restaurant" serving a "big menu" of "authentic, flavorful" fare to a crowd of "mostly locals" who "like it really spicy"; "reasonable prices" are another reason the "small attached parking lot fills up quickly", but fortunately, "takeout is an option."

Cholo's Homestyle Mexican *Mexican* 16 | 15 | 18 | $21

Haleiwa | North Shore Mktpl. | 66-250 Kamehameha Hwy. (bet. Amara Rd. & Kilioe Pl.) | 808-637-3059 | www.cholosmexican.com

"After a day on the North Shore", you "gotta go" to this "popular" Haleiwa Mexican for "surfer-friendly grinds" and "amazing" margaritas; though critics clamor that service can be "slow" because it's "always so busy", the setting's "not exactly fine dining" and the fare is "subpar", many agree that it "will do if you need a fix."

Ciao Mein *Chinese/Italian* 22 | 23 | 24 | $52

Waikiki | Hyatt Regency Waikiki Resort & Spa | 2424 Kalakaua Ave. (Uluniu St.) | Honolulu | 808-923-2426 | www.waikiki.hyatt.com

The "interesting fusion" of Chinese and Italian cuisines at this Hyatt Regency Waikiki eatery "comes off very well" according to fans and is "worth a try", plus it's backed by a "charming atmosphere and outstanding service"; a "wonderful wine list" is a plus, so all in all few complain if it's "expensive."

	FOOD	DECOR	SERVICE	COST

Contemporary Café Ⓜ *American*

FOOD	DECOR	SERVICE	COST
21	21	17	$19

Makiki Heights | The Contemporary Museum | 2411 Makiki Heights Dr. (Mott-Smith Dr.) | Honolulu | 808-523-3362 | www.tcmhi.org

At this American lunch cafe in the Contemporary Museum in Makiki Heights, "outdoor seating", "beautiful gardens" and "views from the lawn" make for a "tranquil, nourishing setting" where you can "get away from it all"; the "limited" menu of "fresh", "healthy" salads, sandwiches and snacks is "surprisingly good for a museum", and cap off a "worthwhile outing" for art aficionados.

DK Steak House *Steak*

FOOD	DECOR	SERVICE	COST
22	19	22	$54

Waikiki | Waikiki Beach Marriott Resort & Spa | 2552 Kalakaua Ave. (bet. Ohua & Paoakalani Aves.) | Honolulu | 808-931-6280 | www.dkrestaurants.com

"Fabulous" dry-aged steaks, a "nice selection of sides" and an "extensive wine list" are served by a "friendly" staff at the Waikiki Beach Marriott's "pricey" steakhouse from D.K. Kodama (of Sansei Seafood fame); some find the decor "lacking" and the scene "loud", but for carnivores it's all about the "awesome" meat.

Downtown @ the HISAM Ⓢ *American*

FOOD	DECOR	SERVICE	COST
24	19	19	$22

Downtown | Hawaii State Art Museum | 250 S. Hotel St. (bet. Alakea & Richards Sts.) | Honolulu | 808-536-5900 | www.state.hi.us/sfca

At this New American "luncheon gem" in the Hawaii State Art Museum, there's "art on the walls and on the plate" in the form of "wonderfully creative", "super-fresh" sandwiches, "quiches made in heaven" and other items that'll "bowl you over", served by a "friendly" staff in an "über-chic cafeteria" setting; gripes about "really high prices" notwithstanding, it's a popular stop for not only visitors but the "Downtown working crowd" too, including "politicians" and even "the Governor"; P.S. it's the sibling of Town in Kaimuki.

Duc's Bistro *French/Vietnamese*

FOOD	DECOR	SERVICE	COST
24	19	23	$43

Chinatown | 1188 Maunakea St. (bet. Beretania & Pauahi Sts.) | Honolulu | 808-531-6325 | www.ducsbistro.com

Duc Nguyen "does magic" at his Chinatown bistro, "rocking palates" with his "beautifully prepared" French-Vietnamese cuisine, which is backed by a "small but well-thought-out wine list"; the "friendly" chef/co-owner "treats guests like family" and oversees a "superbly trained" staff in the "Indochine" setting, where you feel like you're in a "noir movie from the '40s", and though it's "not in the nicest part" of town, most consider it "well worth a visit"; P.S. there's live music at the "correct volume for dinner" twice a week.

Duke's Canoe Club *American* 20 | 23 | 20 | $34

Waikiki | Outrigger Waikiki | 2335 Kalakaua Ave. (bet. Duke's Ln. & Kaiulani Ave.) | Honolulu | 808-922-2268 | www.dukeswaikiki.com

Like a "Hollywood version of Hawaii", this landmark at the Outrigger Waikiki Beach and its Kauai Marriott sibling make you "feel the island spirit" thanks to "gorgeous" locations and "*Fantasy Island*" settings adorned with pictures of the eponymous surfing legend and assorted "beach boys"; "Hawaiian singers" stroll among visitors and locals who "pretend they're on vacation" as they knock back "killer" mai tais and tuck into "dependable" American pub grub served by a "friendly" (some say "amateurish") staff - ok, maybe it's "noisy" and a little "touristy", but it's "still lots of fun."

Eggs 'n Things *American* 22 | 12 | 18 | $18

Waikiki | 343 Saratoga Rd. (Kalakaua Ave.) | Honolulu | 808-923-3447 | www.eggsnthings.com

The "eggcellent" "Hawaiian-style" breakfasts ("mac nut waffles to wallow in", "divine" coconut pancakes) served all day at this Waikiki American are "wonderful" whether you're "hungover or not", even though tabs "can be pricey"; though it's "always packed", the "efficient" staff makes the "tables rotate quickly" and the "new location" (since 2009) "has more room" than the previous address, but many local cognoscenti still "go early" to "avoid the lines" and "tourists."

Ezogiku *Japanese/Noodle Shop* 21 | 11 | 18 | $14

Pearl City | Pearl City Shopping Ctr. | 850 Kamehameha Hwy. (bet. Puu Momi St. & Waimano Home Rd.) | 808-455-2815

Aiea | Waimalu Shopping Ctr. | 98-020 Kamehameha Hwy. (bet. Kaahumanu & Kaonohi Sts.) | 808-488-9850

University | 1010 University Ave. (Beretania St.) | Honolulu | 808-942-3608

Waikiki | 2146 Kalakaua Ave. (Beachwalk) | Honolulu | 808-926-8618

(continued)

Ezogiku

Waikiki | Royal Hawaiian Ctr. | 2201 Kalakaua Ave. (Duke's Ln.) | Honolulu | 808-447-7595
Waikiki | 2420 Koa Ave. (bet. Kaiulani & Uluniu Aves.) | Honolulu | 808-922-2473
www.ezogiku.com

"Japanese tourists", "bar-hoppers", "students" and others flock to these noodle "holes-in-the-wall" for "enormous bowls of ramen" that "never disappoint", plus "great gyoza" and other sides; some sniff there's "nothing special" about them, but fans recommend it "if you want cheap food" and "don't care about how a place looks."

Fat Greek *Greek* 17 | 11 | 15 | $18

Kaimuki | 3040 Waialae Ave. (bet. 1st Ave. & St. Louis Dr.) | Honolulu | 808-734-0404 | www.thefatgreek.net

A "popular student hangout", this "no-frills" Kaimuki Greek offers "tasty" fare "and lots of it" at "moderate prices", and BYO with no corkage makes it an even bigger "bargain"; there's "lots of lively conversation" in the "spartan" digs.

Fook Yuen ◐ *Chinese* 22 | 12 | 16 | $24

McCully | McCully Shopping Ctr. | 1960 Kapiolani Blvd. (bet. McCully & Pumehana Sts.) | Honolulu | 808-973-0168

While wags say the "name alone should draw you inside" this McCully strip-mall spot, "local folks" are hooked instead by the "fantastic" Cantonese fare at "reasonable" prices; reports of "curt" service and "typical Chinese restaurant decor" notwithstanding, it's "always busy", even "late at night" (until 3 AM).

Formaggio Grill *Mediterranean* 21 | 19 | 19 | $35

Kailua | 305 Hahani St. (Kailua Rd.) | 808-263-2633

Formaggio Wine & Cheese Bar ◐ ☒ *Mediterranean*

Kaimuki | Market City Shopping Ctr. | 2919 Kapiolani Blvd. (Harding Ave.) | Honolulu | 808-739-7719
www.formaggio808.com

French-Med "comfort food plus more cutting-edge dishes" and an "extensive", "fairly priced" wine list attract an "urbane" crowd to this oenophile-friendly duo; the Honolulu original "feels like home" to stalwarts who praise its "delicious small plates" "designed to be shared", "knowledgeable" staff and "intimate" setting, while the Kailua sibling can get "noisy" with a "young drinking crowd" and "singles scene."

Genki Sushi *Japanese* 16 | 13 | 16 | $22

Kaneohe | 45-480 Kaneohe Bay Dr. (Kamehameha Hwy.) | 808-247-9595
Pearl City | 98-430 Kamehameha Hwy. (bet. Kaahumanu St. & Kuleana Rd.) | 808-485-0227
Waipahu | Waikele Ctr. | 94-799 Lumiaina St. (Paiwa St.) | 808-678-3180
Ala Moana | Ala Moana Ctr. | 1450 Ala Moana Blvd. (bet. Atkinson Dr. & Piikoi St.) | Honolulu | 808-942-9102
Ewa Beach | 91-1401 Fort Weaver Rd. (Geiger Rd.) | 808-683-1003
Kapahulu | 885 Kapahulu Ave. (Olu St.) | Honolulu | 808-735-7700
Ward | Ward Ctr. | 1200 Ala Moana Blvd. (Kamakee St.) | Honolulu | 808-591-5600
www.genkisushiusa.com

For "quick, affordable sushi", fans head to this Japanese chain serving "all the usual dishes" that you pick off the "little treadmill" as they pass by ("fun for kids"), plus "anything you want can be ordered" from the "friendly" staff; there's usually a "long line" and a few find the fare just "average" and fret about how long it's "been on the conveyor belt", but for many, it's "fast, easy and it satisfies."

Goma Tei Ramen *Japanese/Noodle Shop* 22 | 18 | 20 | $16

Ala Moana | 1425 Ala Moana Blvd. (Atikinson Dr.) | Honolulu | 808-947-9188
Ward | Ward Ctr. | 1200 Ala Moana Blvd. (Kamakee St.) | Honolulu | 808-591-9188

"Comfort on a cold (for Honolulu), rainy night" comes in the form of "chewy ramen and meltingly soft pork" in a "spicy sesame broth" at this affordable Japanese noodle duo in Ala Moana and Ward, while "hot, crusty" gyoza and "cold, refreshing" draft beer also make it "popular among locals and Japanese tourists in the know"; the staff is "helpful", though even so you can "expect to wait for a seat" in the simple but "modern" settings.

	FOOD	DECOR	SERVICE	COST

Green Door Ⓜ *Malaysian/Singaporean* | 22 | 8 | 10 | $23

Chinatown | 1110 Nuuanu Ave. (S. Hotel St.) | Honolulu | 808-533-0606

Aficionados attest the Malaysian-Singaporean fare "will knock your socks off" at this Chinatown "hole-in-the-wall" run by "famously grouchy" chef-owner Betty Pang, where you're "served on paper plates" in a small space with "nonexistent" decor; though some feel that the proprietor "does her best to discourage you from ever going back", diehards keep returning for the "creative", "inexpensive" eats.

Gyotaku *Japanese* | 20 | 15 | 20 | $24

Pearl City | 98-1226 Kaahumanu St. (Moanalua Rd.) | 808-487-0091
Downtown | 1824 S. King St. (Artesian St.) | Honolulu | 808-949-4584
Niu Valley | Niu Valley Shopping Ctr. | 5730 Kalanianaole Hwy. (Halemaumau St.) | Honolulu | 808-373-2731
www.gyotakuhawaii.com

Locals favor this "affordable" Japanese trio for "easy, economical and casual family dinners" thanks to its "large" menu of "well-prepared" "standard" dishes offering "something for everyone"; the servers are "friendly and efficient", though at times can appear "rushed", and while some find the "casual" digs "comfortable", others describe them as "spartan" and "tired"; P.S. the lunch specials are a "fantastic value."

Hakkei Ⓢ Ⓜ *Japanese* | ▽ 26 | 23 | 27 | $46

Makiki | 1436 Young St. (bet. Kalakaua Ave. & Keeaumoku St.) | Honolulu | 808-944-6688 | www.hakkei-honolulu.com

At this "tiny" Makiki Japanese you feel like you're in a "country inn in Japan" thanks to *Iron Chef* winner Seiya Masahara's "excellent, authentic" cuisine and "personable, sincere" service from a staff that "could not be nicer"; purists declare it the "real deal", and while some caution that it may "not be for every palate", overall it's a "delicious adventure in eating."

Hakone Ⓜ *Japanese* | 26 | 23 | 26 | $50

Waikiki | Hawaii Prince Hotel Waikiki | 100 Holomoana St. (Ala Moana Blvd.) | Honolulu | 808-944-4494 | www.princeresortshawaii.com

Even "guests from Japan" are "impressed" by the "excellent" buffet at this "higher-grade" Japanese in the Hawaii Prince Hotel in

Waikiki, which offers a "wide array" of "authentic" dishes, including the "freshest sashimi and sushi", plus shrimp tempura that's "worth the price of admission alone"; service is "subdued" yet "outstanding", and the "quiet" setting offers a "fabulous view of Ala Wai" Harbor.

Haleiwa Eats Thai *Thai* ∇ 24 | 14 | 20 | $23

Haleiwa | 66-079 Kamehameha Hwy. (Haleiwa Rd.) | 808-637-4247 | www.haleiwaeatsthai.com

An "out-of-the-way place" serving "out-of-this-world food" is how devotees describe this "classic North Shore hippie hangout" in Haleiwa, where the "freshly prepared" Thai fare is "exceptional" and the staff is "friendly" and "dedicated"; those who demur at the "noisy", "tile-and-metal dining area" deem it "better for takeout"; it's BYO, with a $7 corkage for wine, $1 for beer.

Hale Vietnam *Vietnamese* 22 | 11 | 18 | $21

Kaimuki | 1140 12th Ave. (bet. Harding & Waialae Aves.) | Honolulu | 808-735-7581

"Pho sure", this veteran Vietnamese has "stood the test of time" according to denizens of Kaimuki, and even though it's a "well-kept local secret", regulars report it's "always crowded" thanks to "wonderful, fresh" and "authentic" fare at "good prices"; aside from a "huge, laughing Buddha" near the front of the room, many find the digs "dreary", while others complain of "inconsistent" service.

Hard Rock Cafe *American* 15 | 20 | 17 | $28

Waikiki | 280 Beachwalk (Kalakaua Ave.) | Honolulu | 808-955-7383 | www.hardrock.com

There's "nothing exactly local" about these links of the "noisy", "nostalgic", music-driven American chain – "except the gorgeous Pacific Ocean" when "you look out the window" at Maui and the "surfboards" on the walls in Oahu; "rock memorabilia" is their claim to fame, and if the food doesn't exactly rock, it's fine for "enjoying a burger and a beer"; yet other than "headbangers", "tourists" and youngsters who "love" those T-shirts, "does anyone still think this is cool?"

	FOOD	DECOR	SERVICE	COST

Hau Tree Lanai *Pacific Rim* 21 27 22 $43

Waikiki | New Otani Kaimana Beach Hotel | 2863 Kalakaua Ave. (Monsarrat Ave.) | Honolulu | 808-921-7066 | www.kaimana.com

Located "on the sand right next to the waves", its tables shaded by the "namesake hau trees", this outdoor eatery in Waikiki's New Otani Kaimana Beach is a "perfect sunset dining spot" and a "great place for a memorable proposal, or to celebrate an anniversary"; "friendly" servers "make you feel like royalty", and if some deem the Pacific Rim seafood "workmanlike", fans find it "delightful" and note that "watching the surf makes it even more tasty."

Helena's Hawaiian Food *Hawaiian* 25 10 19 $18

Kalihi | 1240 N. School St. (Houghtailing St.) | Honolulu | 808-845-8044 | www.helenashawaiianfood.com

The "authentic", "strictly local" Hawaiian "home cooking" at this "friendly" family-run BYO Kalihi "landmark" "will knock you out", and the "unique" "Spanish-Hawaiian-Korean-Japanese-Portuguese-Polynesian mashups" make it a "must" for "adventurous eaters"; sure, the service can be "slow", the food's served on "cafeteria-style plates" at "bare-bones tables" and it's cash-only - but fans insist the "bus' ya mout" fare will ensure that "you won't care" about any of that.

Highway Inn *Diner* 21 13 19 $17

Waipahu | 94-226 Leoku St. (bet. Farrington Hwy. & Waipahu St.) | 808-677-4345 | www.myhighwayinn.com

For "local kine", "onolicious" "Hawaiian diner food" and "plate-lunches", fans recommend this "ohana" Waipahu spot run by three generations of the Toguchi family since 1947; most agree "you're not there for the decor", and some caution that the "down-home" service "can be intimidating for a newcomer", especially one "not from the islands", though many others find it "friendly" and "quick."

Z Hiroshi Eurasion Tapas *Eurasian* 28 23 27 $51

Restaurant Row | 500 Ala Moana Blvd. (bet. Punchbowl & South Sts.) | Honolulu | 808-533-4476 | www.hiroshihawaii.com

Two "masters", chef Hiroshi Fukui and sommelier Chuck Furuya, team up (together with restaurateur D.K. Kodama) at their "major-league" establishment on Restaurant Row, which has achieved "almost cult" status with its "inspired" Eurasian tapas featuring "locally grown products" and "fantastic" wine pairings from a "superb" list, plus "excellent" service in a "quiet, contemporary" setting; happy hour offers some "amazing" deals, and the occasional kaiseki dinners (reservations required) are a "great bargain."

Hoku's *Pacific Rim* 26 | 27 | 26 | $68

Kahala | Kahala Hotel & Resort | 5000 Kahala Ave. (Kealaolu Ave.) | Honolulu | 808-739-8780 | www.kahalaresort.com

"Stunning views" of the Pacific from an "oceanside" location and "elegant, contemporary" decor create a "romantic" tableau at the Kahala Hotel's "special-occasion" Pacific Rim establishment offering "top-notch" fare, including what some call the "best brunch on the beach in Oahu", and "exceptional" service; despite grumbles about "hotel prices" and "stuffy" taboos on "resort wear", most consider it an "excellent choice."

Hula Grill Waikiki *Pacific Rim* 21 | 23 | 21 | $36

Waikiki | Outrigger Waikiki | 2335 Kalakaua Ave. (bet. Duke's Ln. & Kaiulani Ave.) | Honolulu | 808-923-4852 | www.hulagrillwaikiki.com

"Fantabulous" sunsets, "sand in your toes, mai tai in hand" and "locally caught" "fresh fish" - "nothing can beat it" exclaim enthusiasts of this oceanside Pacific Rim duo in the Outrigger Waikiki and on Kaanapali Beach; some may find the land-based offerings merely "adequate", but service is generally "very good" even when it's "busy", and the Oahu location offers "people-watching at its best", especially "later in the evening" when things "get a bit rowdy."

Hy's Steak House *Steak* 26 | 25 | 27 | $60

Waikiki | Waikiki Park Heights Hotel | 2440 Kuhio Ave. (Uluniu Ave.) | Honolulu | 808-922-5555 | www.hyshawaii.com

Devotees promise an "unforgettable dining experience" at this "high-end steakhouse" in the Waikiki Park Heights Hotel that's like a "gentlemen's eating club", with "superb" "white-glove" service from waiters in "tuxedos", "fabulous" steaks "cooked to perfection" and "tableside preparations of Caesar salads", plus retro "flambé desserts"; "overstuffed chairs", "leather booths" and a "Tiffany stained-glass ceiling" highlight the "formal", "throwback" setting, and while it's not cheap, many say it's "worth breaking the bank one time" for a "special occasion."

Ichiriki Japanese Nabe *Japanese* 24 | 20 | 22 | $34

Ala Moana | 510 Piikoi St. (bet. Hopaka & Kona Sts.) | Honolulu | 808-589-2299

The signature nabe "warms the soul" at this Ala Moana Japanese where "you cook your own" "addictive" hotpot or "tasty" shabu-shabu over "relaxed conversation" in an "authentic", "contemporary" setting; add in a "friendly" staff that "aims to please" with "fast" service, and it's an "outstanding" experience overall, but cognoscenti advise wearing "cool, airy clothes" because it can feel like a "sauna."

Indigo ⊠ Ⓜ *Asian* 21 | 23 | 21 | $44

Chinatown | 1121 Nuuanu Ave. (Hotel St.) | Honolulu | 808-521-2900 | www.indigo-hawaii.com

The "exotic" decor adds a "touch of romance" to the "memorable layout" of various "themed rooms" at this "popular spot" in Chinatown; the "interesting" "Asian fusion flavors really sizzle", the lunch buffet is "outstanding" and service is "very friendly", and though a few critics find it "overpriced", for most it's a "refreshing option" convenient to the Hawaii Theater and nearby art galleries.

Island's Fine Burgers *Burgers* 19 | 18 | 19 | $18

Ala Moana | Ala Moana Ctr. | 1450 Ala Moana Blvd. (bet. Atkinson Dr. & Piikoi St.) | Honolulu | 808-943-6670 | www.islandsrestaurants.com

For "tasty burgers and endless fries" at "good prices", this "reliable" Ala Moana link of the West Coast chain "never disappoints", and the "lava cake with vanilla ice cream" is a "must for dessert"; while it's a "fun place for the family", it also offers an "awesome happy hour", and "big-screen TVs" make it a popular venue on "game days and nights."

Jameson's By The Sea *Seafood/Steak* 19 | 20 | 21 | $39

Haleiwa | 62-540 Kamehameha Hwy. (Haleiwa Rd.) | 808-637-4336 | www.jamesonshawaii.com

"Spectacular views" of the ocean from a "fabulous location" "across the road" from Haleiwa Beach have made this surf 'n' turf "standby" a "North Shore favorite" for three decades, where the staff provides "lovely" service "with local knowledge and a smile"; though detractors deride it as an "overpriced "tour-bus special" serving "so-so" fare, defenders counter that you "can't go wrong" with the "locally caught fish" followed by "drinks on the deck at sunset."

Jimmy Buffett's at the Beachcomber ◐ *American* 18 | 20 | 20 | $29

Waikiki | Ohana Waikiki Beachcomber | 2300 Kalakaua Ave. (Duke's Ln.) | Honolulu | 808-791-1200 | www.jimmybuffettsatthebeachcomber.com

"Margaritaville in Hawaii" can be found at this "theme" American in the Ohana Waikiki Beachcomber, a "tourists' paradise" with a "beachy", "laid-back vibe" where "loops of Jimmy Buffett" play on a "huge video screen", free live music adds to the "party atmosphere" and you can "feel the breeze on the rooftop patio"; "friendly, helpful" service helps make up for "average" eats, but critics are cool to the "loud" spectacle of "too many parrot heads having too many drinks."

Kaka'ako Kitchen *Hawaiian* 22 | 10 | 15 | $16

Ward | Ward Ctr. | 1200 Ala Moana Blvd. (Kamakee St.) | Honolulu | 808-594-3663 | www.wardcenters.com

"Gourmet plate lunches" is not an "oxymoron" at 3660 chef-owner Russell Siu's affordable Hawaiian "conveniently" located in the Ward Center, where your "fancy meal in a Styrofoam box" represents "high-end restaurant quality" at "fast-food prices"; service is "quick" because you "order and take a number" at the counter, and while you can eat at one of the "outdoor tables", most use it for "takeout."

Keo's in Waikiki *Thai* 22 | 21 | 21 | $38

Waikiki | 2028 Kuhio Ave. (bet. Keoniana & Kuamoo Sts.) | Honolulu | 808-951-9355 | www.keosthaicuisine.com

"Nobody beats the spring rolls" at Keo Sananikone's "popular" Waikiki Thai offering "innovative, fresh" Siamese dishes, such as the "delectable" signature Evil Jungle Prince entree, ferried by "friendly" servers; opinions are split on the "over-the-top rococo" space featuring "bronze statues" and "massive tropical flower arrangements" - what's "garish" to some is "fun" to others - and while a few critics say it's heading "downhill", the fact that it's "always full" says a lot.

Kincaid's *Seafood/Steak* 20 | 19 | 21 | $35

Ward | Ward Warehouse | 1050 Ala Moana Blvd. (Ward Ave.) | Honolulu | 808-591-2005 | www.kincaids.com

"Superb fresh seafood", "nicely prepared" steaks and "delicious" salads come with a view of Kewalo Basin at this surf 'n' turf chain link in Ward Warehouse, a "reliable", "anytime kind of place" where "locals" head for "power lunches", "family gatherings" or to "meet their next mates"; "friendly" service is another plus, and even if there's "no wow factor", fans deem it "always satisfactory for what it is."

Kirin ◐ *Chinese* 23 | 15 | 18 | $30

Moiliili | 2518 S. Beretania St. (Bingham St.) | Honolulu | 808-942-1888

Sinophiles "can never pass up" the dim sum at this "off-the-beaten-path" Moiliili Chinese that attracts "visitors and locals" alike, serving up "authentic" fare "with a spin", including "dishes not normally seen on Honolulu menus"; "very nice" service helps make up for "limited parking."

Kobe Japanese Steak House & Sushi Bar ◐ *Japanese* 22 | 18 | 21 | $42

Waikiki | 1841 Ala Moana Blvd. (Kalia Rd.) | Honolulu | 808-941-4444 | www.honolulukobe.com

The "first choice" of many a fan of "flames and knives", this "affordable" teppanyaki duo in Lahaina and Waikiki provides "exciting entertainment" and "fresh", "flavorful" grilled fare that's "better than the norm", plus "consistent" sushi; a few critics clamor about "long waits" and "smoky" conditions, but lots of locals laud them as "reliable places to take out-of-towners."

Kona Brewing Co. *American* 20 | 19 | 19 | $26

Hawaii Kai | Koko Marina Ctr. | 7192 Kalanianaole Hwy. (Lunalilo Home Rd.) | Honolulu | 808-394-5662 | www.konabrewingco.com

See review in Big Island Directory.

Kozo Sushi *Japanese* 20 | 12 | 19 | $16

Pearl City | 1029 Makolu St. (Kuala Rd.) | 808-455-6805
Aiea | Pearlridge Ctr. Downtown | 98-1005 Moanalua Rd. (Kamehameha Hwy.) | 808-483-6805
Kahala | Kahala Mall | 4618 Kilauea Ave. (Pahoa Ave.) | Honolulu | 808-733-5733
Kapahulu | 625 Kapahulu Ave. (Mooheau St.) | Honolulu | 808-739-2785
Moiliili | 2334 S. King St. (bet. Hoawa Ln. & Isenberg St.) | Honolulu | 808-951-5696
www.kozosushihawaii.net

"Kamaaina seem to love" this "to-go" sushi chain for its "nice variety" of "ono" rolls, and the "helpful" staff strives to ensure "short waits for takeout"; whether you're "picking up a meal for the beach or the plane" or a "good-value" party platter, boosters boast it's "cheap" and "quick."

Kua 'Aina Sandwich *Burgers/Sandwiches* 22 | 13 | 16 | $14

Haleiwa | 66-160 Kamehameha Hwy. (Haleiwa Rd.) | 808-637-6067
Ward | Ward Ctr. | 1200 Ala Moana Blvd. (Kamakee St.) | Honolulu | 808-591-9133

Every "now and then your health can afford" the "sloppy", "artery-clogging" hamburgers, "excellent" "gourmet" sandwiches and "matchstick" fries "to die for" at this Oahu duo; fans praise the "family-friendly" ambiance of the original "shack" in Haleiwa and the "strip-mall" sibling in the Ward Center, and though service gets mixed reports ("fast or slow" and sometimes "rude"), patty addicts consider it "a must."

Z La Mer *French* 28 | 29 | 28 | $98

Waikiki | Halekulani | 2199 Kalia Rd. (Lewers St.) | Honolulu | 808-923-2311 | www.halekulani.com

"They make you feel like a big kahuna" at the Halekulani Hotel's "formal" French restaurant, voted Hawaii's No. 1 for Decor and Service, where you can hear the "sound of waves" and "Hawaiian music from the shore" in the "gorgeous, open-air room overlooking Waikiki Beach" as an "attentive" staff serves "amazing" Gallic cuisine with "subtle Asian accents" and selections from a "superb" wine list; sure, you'll "spend a fortune", but many insist it's "worth the splurge"; jackets required.

Z Le Bistro *French* 27 | 20 | 25 | $55

Niu Valley | Niu Valley Shopping Ctr. | 5730 Kalanianaole Hwy. (Halemaumau St.) | Honolulu | 808-373-7990

Alan and Debbie Takasaki "make dining magic" at their Niu Valley "surprise for Francophiles", a "romantic retreat in a strip mall" where "balanced and beautiful" French cuisine "with Hawaiian flair" plus "excellent" service attract a "stimulating cross section of diners", including "lots of locals"; a few feel "cramped" in the "quiet, unassuming" space, especially when it gets "crowded", but just about all agree it's "worth a visit if not a detour."

Little Village Noodle House *Chinese* 23 | 16 | 19 | $22

Chinatown | 1113 Smith St. (N. Hotel St.) | Honolulu | 808-545-3008 | www.littlevillagehawaii.com

It may indeed be "little" (with a "tiny" kitchen), but this Chinatown "winner" is "big on flavors and aromas" attest fans who come for "huge portions" of "creative", "inexpensive" Chinese fare; there's "always a long line", but the "friendly" servers "are quick - sometimes too quick" - and though "you need to speak up in conversations" amid the "bustling" scene, it's nonetheless a "fun place to go with friends."

Longhi's *Italian* 21 | 20 | 20 | $44

Ala Moana | Ala Moana Ctr. | 1450 Ala Moana Blvd. (bet. Atkinson Dr. & Piikoi St.) | Honolulu | 808-947-9899 | www.longhis.com

See review in Maui Directory.

Lucy's Grill 'N Bar *Eclectic* 21 | 17 | 18 | $36

Kailua | 33 Aulike St. (bet. Kuulei Rd. & Uluniu St.) | 808-230-8188

"Not your run-of-the-mill grill", this Kailua Eclectic comes as a "surprise" to some with its "perfectly prepared and presented" seafood, "big, juicy" meats and "great selection" of wines, all served in a "delightful", "lively" setting; cognoscenti advise the "outdoor seating area is quieter than indoors", where the "noise" can be "overpowering", and while the staff is "very friendly" with "regulars" (and "the Obamas"), some newcomers report being treated like "second-class citizens."

MAC 24/7 ◐ *American* 19 | 19 | 17 | $24

Waikiki | Hilton Waikiki Prince Kuhio | 2500 Kuhio Ave. (Liliuokalani Ave.) | Honolulu | 808-921-5564 | www.mac247hawaii.com

Whether you're a "big eater with something to prove" or you just "love to eat pancakes", this "hip" diner in the Hilton Waikiki Prince Kuhio may be the "place to feed your appetite", with flapjacks "the size of pizzas", as well as "jumbo" portions of "awesome" chicken and waffles and other comfort-food offerings; "friendly" servers man the "modern" digs that remind some of an "upscale gym", and its 24/7 operations make it a popular stop for many "after a drunken night."

Mariposa *American* 23 | 24 | 23 | $45

Ala Moana | Neiman Marcus, Ala Moana Ctr. | 1450 Ala Moana Blvd. (bet. Atkinson Dr. & Piikoi St.) | Honolulu | 808-951-3420 | www.neimanmarcus.com

For a "business lunch" or an "upscale" shopping break, fans head to this "oasis" atop Neiman Marcus in the Ala Moana Center to enjoy its "beautiful setting" "overlooking the park and the ocean" and "ample" menu of "well-prepared" New American fare (including "fabulous" popovers); the ambiance is "high-class but comfortable" and the service is "attentive", but some find it "a little pricey for what you get"; P.S. "be sure to park on the makai side (ocean side) if you go for dinner", as the store closes before the restaurant.

Z Matsumoto's Shave Ice *Dessert* 23 | 11 | 18 | $6

Haleiwa | 66-087 Kamehameha Hwy. (bet. Haleiwa & Opaeula Rds.) | 808-637-4827 | www.matsumotoshaveice.com

For those who think Hawaii means "sun, sand, surf and shave ice", this Haleiwa "hole-in-the-wall" "icon" - voted the state's Best Buy - is "one of the bucket list things to do" on the North Shore, dishing out "tropical slushy goodness" flavored with an "unmatched variety" of syrups, plus extras such as "ice cream on the bottom" or "azuki beans and condensed milk"; "don't let the long line scare you" because it "moves fast", thanks to a staff that's "good with clueless tourists."

Maui Tacos *Mexican* 19 | 8 | 14 | $13

Kailua | Kailua Village Shops | 539 Kailua Rd. (Hahani St.) | 808-261-4155

Waikiki | Royal Hawaiian Ctr. | 2233 Kalakaua Ave. (Royal Hawaiian Ave.) | Honolulu | 808-931-6111

www.mauitacos.com

See review in Maui Directory.

Mediterraneo ☒ *Italian* ▽ 24 | 18 | 19 | $32

Makiki | 1279 S. King St. (bet. Akala Ln. & Akoko St.) | Honolulu | 808-593-1466

"Big portions" of "wonderful" Italian fare, including "divine seafood", are the draw at this Makiki trattoria, where "personal" service from the chef and a "warm, cozy family atmosphere" help make up for the "small" (some say "nondescript") space; the "ambitious" menu is deemed "totally worth the wait and the time it takes to find parking."

Mekong Thai II *Thai* 21 | 15 | 18 | $28

Ala Moana | 1726 S. King St. (bet. Elsle & Pawaa Lns.) | Honolulu | 808-941-6212

Fans insist you "can't go wrong" with the "tasty" Siamese fare at this Ala Moana spot that's usually "full of regulars" who are hooked on the "consistent", "genuine" eats; "attentive" service helps many overlook the "simple" surroundings, and while a few feel it's "just not the same" as its late Moiliili sibling, others tout it as a "best buy if you like Thai."

Z Michel's *French* 27 | 27 | 27 | $74

Waikiki | Colony Surf | 2895 Kalakaua Ave. (Poni Moi Rd.) | Honolulu | 808-923-6552 | www.michelshawaii.com

For a "sumptuous", "old-school" dining experience, "locals and tourists" alike head to this "legendary" Waikiki "warhorse" whose "beautiful location right on the beach" provides "unmatched" views of "awesome sunsets" and the "city lights" at night; "skilled, tuxedoed waiters do all sorts of tableside preparations" while serving "superb" Classic French cuisine in a "semi-alfresco" setting that makes "indoors seem like outdoors" – many just "don't want the evening to end" (or the check to arrive).

Mix Café ⊠ *Italian/Sandwiches* 21 | 11 | 18 | $11

Downtown | 1025 Alakea St. (bet. Hotel & King Sts.) | Honolulu | 808-532-4540

Downtown | 35 S. Beretania St. (Bethel St.) | Honolulu | 808-537-1191

www.mymixcafe.com

"Beneath a simple surface lies a depth of flavor rarely encountered in Honolulu" rhapsodize fans of this Italian cafe duo that attracts the "Downtown lunch crowd" and "university students" with "amazing sandwiches", "yummy" salads and other "fresh-cooked" fare; a few frown at the "cost" and "skimpy" servings, but others find it "reasonably priced" for the quality and "satisfying."

NEW Morimoto Waikiki *Japanese* - | - | - | VE

Waikiki | Waikiki Edition Hotel | 1775 Ala Moana Blvd. (Hobron Ln.) | Honolulu | 808-943-5900 | www.morimotowaikiki.com

Iron Chef Masaharu Morimoto's newest venture in the posh Waikiki Edition Hotel showcases his signature Western-influenced Japanese cuisine, including a seven-course omakase menu, in a sleek, island-themed space by Thomas Schoos that features an open kitchen and a semi-private dining room enclosed in sheer curtains; you can take in views of the ocean and a nearby yacht club from the open-air lanai, which boasts plush sofas and two fire pits.

Morton's The Steakhouse *Steak* 24 | 23 | 23 | $68

Ala Moana | Ala Moana Ctr. | 1450 Ala Moana Blvd. (bet. Atkinson Dr. & Piikoi St.) | Honolulu | 808-949-1300 | www.mortons.com

While it's "hardly Hawaii" and there's "no view", this Ala Moana link of the "big-ticket" steakhouse chain "always delivers" "excellently prepared" cuts of beef and "grand sides" "served professionally" in a "high *maka maka*" setting; some find it a bit "staid" and wish they'd "lose the raw-meat presentation" and "high" wine pricing, but the many who love its "traditional" ways consider it "one of the best."

Nico's at Pier 38 ⊠ *Seafood* 25 | 10 | 16 | $15

Kalihi | Pier 38 | 1133 N. Nimitz Hwy. (Alakawa St.) | Honolulu | 808-540-1377 | www.nicospier38.com

Think "food truck at the fishing docks - minus the truck" to picture this "unassuming" all-day takeout "adjacent to the fish auction house" in Iwilei offering "fantastic", "fresh" seafood "right off the boats", "awesome gourmet plate lunches" and breakfast fare, all at prices "too good to be true"; you "order at the counter", then take your meal to outdoor "plastic picnic tables" with a view of the "industrial harbor", and while you can "expect to wait in line", aficionados assure it "moves pretty quick."

Z Nobu Waikiki *Japanese/Peruvian* 27 | 25 | 24 | $73

Waikiki | Waikiki Parc Hotel | 2233 Helumoa Rd. (Lewers St.) | Honolulu | 808-237-6999 | www.noburestaurants.com

"Nobu at his best" is how fans describe the "fabulous" Waikiki Parc Hotel outpost of his "far-reaching empire", where "creative", "memorable" Japanese-Peruvian fusion fare, including "superb" sushi, is served in a "beautiful space" teeming with "beautiful people", including a fair share of "local celebs and actors"; service is "excellent" if a "little stiff" to some, and though a few dissenters find the experience "not as mind-blowing as you'd expect" given the name and "price tag", but by most accounts it's a "wow!"

Oceanarium *American/Seafood* 17 | 24 | 18 | $34

Waikiki | Pacific Beach Hotel | 2490 Kalakaua Ave. (bet. Kealohilani Ave. & Liliuokalani Ave.) | Honolulu | 808-921-6111 | www.pacificbeachhotel.com

For a "unique dining experience", try watching "scuba divers feeding" "sharks and other denizens of the sea" in an "awesome" three-story aquarium at the Pacific Beach Hotel's American seafooder in Waikiki, which serves "reasonable" buffets from morning to night; while some cite "excellent choices" others feel the "food could be better", ditto the service, but either way the water show is "wonderful fun."

Ocean House *Pacific Rim/Seafood* 24 | 25 | 22 | $45

Waikiki | Outrigger Reef on the Beach | 2169 Kalia Rd. (bet. Beachwalk & Saratoga Rd.) | Honolulu | 808-923-2277 | www.oceanhousewaikiki.com

You "can't beat the view" at this open-air Pacific Rim spot at the Outrigger Reef Hotel on Waikiki Beach, whose location and "elegant", "plantation-house" setting make it a "great venue to enjoy fresh seafood" and "strong cocktails"; some find the service only "so-so" by comparison, but overall fans find it a "wonderful place to take out-of-town guests."

	FOOD	DECOR	SERVICE	COST
Okonomiyaki Chibo *Japanese*	▽ 21	18	20	$44

Waikiki | Royal Hawaiian Ctr. | 2201 Kalakaua Ave. (Kanekapolei St.) | Honolulu | 808-922-9722 | www.chibohawaii.com

A popular stop for hard-core Japanophiles and "Japanese tourists" with "cravings for authentic, casual" tastes of home, this outpost of the Osaka okonomiyaki chain in the Waikiki Royal Hawaiian Center offers "delicious" "savory pancakes" and teppanyaki fare; some warn that you might "smell like a greasy spoon upon your departure" given the grilling that's done in front of you, but admirers call it an "excellent dining experience" nonetheless.

Ola *Hawaii Reg.* 21 | 25 | 19 | $41

Kahuku | Turtle Bay Resort | 57-091 Kamehameha Hwy. (Kuilima Dr.) | 808-293-0801 | www.olaislife.com

Its "beautiful location" "right on the beach" and "spectacular" views of the coast are the stuff of "dreams" for fans of this hotel Hawaii Regional at the North Shore's Turtle Bay Resort; dishes featuring "local ingredients" are "competently prepared" and "attractively presented", and the service is "fine", but some find the fare merely "average" and recommend it only for "drinks and apps."

Olive Tree Café *Greek* 25 | 11 | 17 | $20

Kahala | 4614 Kilauea Ave. (Pahoa Ave.) | Honolulu | 808-737-0303

Even though most "tourists don't find this place", cognoscenti counsel "go early, or you'll be waiting for a table" at this "ever-popular" BYO Greek in Kahala that dishes out "large portions" of "fantastic" Hellenic fare, including souvlaki made with "auction-fresh" fish, "at a low cost"; it's an "informal" scene where you "order at the counter" and grab an outdoor table "next to a parking lot", but for many who find the "waits and crowds a little crazy", "takeout is the preferred method."

Ono Hawaiian Foods *Hawaiian* 25 | 9 | 19 | $19

Kapahulu | 726 Kapahulu Ave. (Kamuela Ave.) | Honolulu | 808-737-2275

The "lau lau is wow-wow" at this family-run Kapahulu "institution" turning out "loving preparations" of "amazing" Hawaiian "soul food" "not made pretty or trendy for tourists", which many call the "best in town"; the "friendly" staff does its best, but "you'll probably have to stand in line" outside the "unremarkable" "shack", so "wear comfortable shoes" and remember, "you're not there for the ambiance"; it's cash-only, and no alcohol is permitted.

Z Orchids *Pacific Rim* 26 | 28 | 27 | $65

Waikiki | Halekulani | 2199 Kalia Rd. (Lewers St.) | Honolulu | 808-923-2311 | www.halekulani.com

A "magical setting" with "breathtaking views of Diamond Head" and what some call the "best Sunday brunch in all of Waikiki" are the highlights of this "classy" open-air Pacific Rim seafooder in the Halekulani Hotel, where you're regaled by the "sound of waves" and evening "live music on the lawn" in the "elegantly Hawaiian" room "overflowing with orchids"; the service is "friendly and gracious" while the "sophisticated" fare is "extraordinary", thus many concur it's "such a fine-dining experience, you hardly notice the price."

Original Pancake House *American* 21 | 11 | 19 | $17

Ala Moana | 1221 Kapiolani Blvd. (bet. Pensacola St. & Piikoi St.) | Honolulu | 808-596-8213

Kapalama | Waikamilo Shopping Plaza | 1414 Dillingham Blvd. (bet. McNeil St. & Waiakamilo Rd.) | Honolulu | 808-847-1496
www.originalpancakehouse.com

Pancakes to "write home about", "eggs in all permutations" and a "huge variety of other breakfast foods" attract "long lines" to this "friendly" pair of Honolulu links in the national coffee-shop chain; the "old-school" decor "doesn't look like much" to some, and others feel it's "lost its shine", but loyalists "hope it never changes."

Outback Steakhouse *Steak* 18 | 16 | 19 | $33

Kapolei | 302 Kamokila Blvd. (bet. Kalaeloa Blvd. & Uluohia St.) | 808-674-1300

Waipahu | Waipio Shopping Ctr. | 94-810 Ukee St. (Oil Loop) | 808-671-7200

Hawaii Kai | 6650 Kalanianaole Hwy. (Portlock Rd.) | Honolulu | 808-396-7576

Waikiki | 1765 Ala Moana Blvd. (Hobron Ln.) | Honolulu | 808-951-6274
www.outback.com

"Reliable" (if "not prime") seasoned steaks provide "real value for the dollar" at this "Aussie-themed" chain where folks love to "overindulge in the bloomin' onion"; it's too "kitschy" and "packaged" for some and the "cute" service is "hit-or-miss", but "you can take all of your kids" since you'll blend right into the "noisy" surroundings.

Paesano *Italian* 20 | 18 | 21 | $32

Aiea | 98-1277 Kaahumanu St. (bet. Kamehameha Hwy. & Moanalua Rd.) | 808-485-8883
Manoa | Manoa Mktpl. | 2752 Woodlawn Dr. (Manoa Rd.) | Honolulu | 808-988-5923
www.paesanohawaii.com

"Consistent, if not spectacular" Italian fare, including "perfectly cooked" pastas, and "friendly", "attentive" service are the calling cards of this "pleasant" pair in Aiea and Manoa, and "reasonable" prices add to their "value"; the "comfortable" settings "mirror each other", and while some say they're "not destination restaurants", many regard them as "nice places for a spur of the moment" meal.

Pagoda Floating Restaurant M *Eclectic* 17 | 19 | 18 | $30

Ala Moana | Pagoda Hotel | 1525 Rycroft St. (Ahana St.) | Honolulu | 808-948-8356 | www.pagodahotel.com

"Hundreds of huge koi" in a "giant" pond, teahouses and a waterfall are highlights of the "beautiful surroundings" at this "affordable" Eclectic in Ala Moana's Pagoda Hotel offering breakfast and dinner buffets of "traditional 'neighborhood' food"; though some feel it's "past its prime", others consider it "well worth the cost", particularly the "great-value" Sunday brunch; it serves dinner Wednesdays-Sundays, breakfast and brunch on Sundays only.

Pah Ke's Chinese Restaurant *Chinese* 22 | 12 | 22 | $21

Kaneohe | 46-018 Kamehameha Hwy. (bet. Kahuhipa & Mehana Sts.) | 808-235-4505 | www.pahke.com

Owned by a former bakery chef, this Kaneohe Sino spot is something of a "rarity among Chinese restaurants", offering "desserts to die for" to top off a "reasonably priced" and "varied" menu of "healthy", "fresh" dishes both "classic" and "unconventional", which are served by a "friendly", "efficient" staff in a "simple", "cafe"-like setting; though some critics find its lack of consistency "frustrating", many "locals" consider it "worth the drive."

Panya Bakery Express Ⓢ *French/Japanese* 21 | 17 | 16 | $19

Downtown | 711 Queen St. (bet. Cooke & Coral Sts.) | Honolulu | 808-597-8880

Panya Bistro *French/Japanese*

Ala Moana | Ala Moana Ctr. | 1450 Ala Moana Blvd. (bet. Atkinson Dr. & Piikoi St.) | Honolulu | 808-946-6388

Downtown | Remington College, lower arcade | 1111 Bishop St. (S. Hotel St.) | Honolulu | 808-536-8363 Ⓢ

Waikiki | Royal Hawaiian Ctr. | 2233 Kalakaua Ave. (Royal Hawaiian Ave.) | Honolulu | 808-791-2969

www.panyabakery.com

Loyalists of this French-Japanese bakery/bistro mini-chain "love, love, love" the "grab-a-quick-bite" menu of "wonderful noodle dishes", "healthy" soups, the "best laksa" and "interesting pastries"; the "trendy" ambiance reminds some of "Ginza in Tokyo", but the "hit-or-miss service" "needs to be tweaked a bit."

Pavilion Café Ⓢ Ⓜ *Mediterranean* ▽ 24 | 20 | 21 | $25

Ala Moana | Honolulu Academy of Arts | 900 S. Beretania St. (bet. Victoria St. & Ward Ave.) | Honolulu | 808-532-8734 | www.honoluluacademy.org

The "outstanding" courtyard setting and "civilized" service are highlights of this "lovely little" "gem" in the Honolulu Academy of Arts in Ala Moana, where museumgoers lunch on reasonably priced, "surprisingly" impressive Asian-influenced Mediterranean fare; it's "one of the best places" for a midday meal say locals, so "make reservations" or "trust your luck."

P.F. Chang's China Bistro *Chinese* 19 | 21 | 21 | $32

Ala Moana | Hokua | 1288 Ala Moana Blvd. (bet. Kamakee & Piikoi Sts.) | Honolulu | 808-596-4710

Waikiki | Royal Hawaiian Ctr. | 2201 Kalakaua Ave (Kanekapolei St.) | Honolulu | 808-628-6760

www.pfchangshawaii.com

"Light, delicious", "Americanized" Chinese food including "standout" lettuce wraps and "many island fusion dishes" keep fans "coming back" to this "trendy", "stylish" nationwide chain with two Oahu links; though not everyone is convinced ("overpriced", "ordinary", "loud"), the "consistent" service is a plus, as is the "smart" menu "catering to people with allergies" and other needs.

Phuket Thai *Thai* 23 | 17 | 20 | $25

Mililani | Town Center Of Mililani | 95-1249 Meheula Pkwy. (bet. Lanikuhana Ave. & Makaimoimo St.) | 808-623-6228
McCully | McCully Shopping Ctr. | 1960 Kapiolani Blvd. (bet. McCully & Pumehana Sts.) | Honolulu | 808-942-8194
Ward | 401 Kamakee St. (bet. Kawaiahao & Queen Sts.) | Honolulu | 808-591-8421
www.phuketthaihawaii.com

Serving "fantastic" Thai fare with the option to take dishes "up a notch" in spiciness, this chainlet trio wins raves; there's "not much decor" in the original McCully location, and the Mililani staff seems "stressed out" to some, so "take out" or head for the "better parking" and larger, sleeker, "less crowded" space at Ward.

Pineapple Room *Hawaii Reg.* 24 | 18 | 22 | $38

Ala Moana | Macy's, Ala Moana Ctr. | 1450 Ala Moana Blvd. (bet. Atkinson Dr. & Piikoi St.) | Honolulu | 808-945-6573 | www.alanwongs.com

Alan Wong's Hawaii Regional at the Ala Moana Center takes "a smaller hit on the wallet" than his flagship, but offers similar "inspired" fare; the staff "makes you feel comfortable" in the bright, "chic" space, adding to the "elegant" experience.

Prince Court *American/Pacific Rim* 22 | 21 | 22 | $43

Waikiki | Hawaii Prince Hotel Waikiki | 100 Holomoana St. (Hobron Ln.) | Honolulu | 808-944-4494 | www.princeresortshawaii.com

The "extensive" buffet, including a "legendary Sunday brunch", is the main event at this New American-Pacific Rim venue in Waikiki, where the offerings range "from prime rib to Japanese"; a "lovely" "view overlooking the marina" and "personable" service are further draws.

Rokkaku *Japanese* ▽ 24 | 22 | 21 | $52

Ala Moana | Ala Moana Ctr. | 1450 Ala Moana Blvd. (bet. Atkinson Dr. & Piikoi St.) | Honolulu | 808-946-3355 | www.rokkak.com

A "high-end", "serene" space elevates this Ala Moana Center Japanese, where "expert chefs" craft an "excellent", if "expensive", menu of contemporary twists on Kyoto-style cuisine; a "helpful" staff seals the deal, though its mall location is "not appealing" to some.

Romano's Macaroni Grill *Italian* 17 17 18 $29

Ala Moana | Ala Moana Ctr. | 1450 Ala Moana Blvd. (bet. Atkinson Dr. & Piikoi St.) | Honolulu | 808-356-8300 | www.macaronigrill.com

There's "much more than macaroni" at these "family-friendly" Italian chain links in Ala Moana and the Waikoloa Resort's Queens' Marketplace; fans of the "steady" lineup of reasonably priced, "fattening" dishes "could eat here every day", but those who deem it "totally generic" with "less-than-zero island ambiance" reserve it "for kids" and the "unadventurous traveler."

Round Table Pizza *Pizza* 19 11 15 $19

Kailua | 1020 Keolu Dr. (bet. Hele & Hui Sts.) | 808-261-4644
Waikiki | Ohana East Hotel | 150 Kaiulani Ave. (Kalakaua Ave.) | Honolulu | 808-944-1199 ◐
Waikiki | Hilton Hawaiian Vill. | 2005 Kalia Rd. (Ala Moana Blvd.) | Honolulu | 808-955-0137 ◐
www.roundtablepizza.com

If you need a "night off from fancy sit-down food" or just a fix of "comfort pizza", piezanos recommend these Maui and Oahu links of the national chain, which offer a "wide selection" of pies served by a "cool", "courteous" staff; while they don't wow everyone ("subpar", "overpriced"), many find them "perfectly acceptable" and a "good deal for a family."

Z Roy's *Hawaii Reg.* 26 22 24 $55

Kapolei | Ko Olina Resort & Marina | 92-1220 Aliinui Dr. (Kamoana Pl.) | 808-676-7697
Hawaii Kai | 6600 Kalanianaole Hwy. (Keahole St.) | Honolulu | 808-396-7697
Waikiki | Waikiki Beach Walk | 226 Lewers St. (Kalia Rd.) | Honolulu | 808-923-7697
www.roysrestaurant.com

Showcasing celeb chef Roy Yamaguchi's "modern mastery" of Hawaii Regional cuisine, this "high-end" nationwide chain (which originated with the Hawaii Kai location) earns the state's Most Popular honors thanks to "creatively prepared" fish, "unique" local specialties and other "fantastic" fare coupled with "excellent" service; if the decor is "looking a little too '90s" for some, that doesn't deter fans who say "every meal is a delight" and worth the "noise" and "crowds"; P.S. you "must have the chocolate molten lava cake."

RumFire *Pacific Rim* 20 | 25 | 17 | $35

Waikiki | Sheraton Waikiki | 2255 Kalakaua Ave. (Royal Hawaiian Ave.) | Honolulu | 808-922-4422 | www.rumfirewaikiki.com

The sunset views "overlooking the ocean" are "unbeatable" at this "cool" venue in the Sheraton Waikiki, where the "fabulous" decor includes floor-to-ceiling windows and "outdoor fire pits"; although the Pacific Rim tapas-style menu doesn't equal the ambiance, it's "creative" enough, especially when complemented by an "impressive rum list" (100 types) and some of the "best" live music.

Ruth's Chris Steak House *Steak* 25 | 22 | 25 | $63

Restaurant Row | 500 Ala Moana Blvd. (bet. Punchbowl & South Sts.) | Honolulu | 808-599-3860

Waikiki | Waikiki Beach Walk | 226 Lewers St. (Kalakaua Ave.) | Honolulu | 808-440-7910

www.ruthschris.com

When "you're tired of fish", it's "hard to go wrong" at any of the Hawaii links in this national chophouse chain, where "sizzling platters" of "buttery steaks" and "winning sides" are delivered by an "impeccable" staff; reviewers single out the two Maui locations for special praise, and advise "taking advantage of the early-bird special."

Sam Choy's Breakfast, Lunch & Crab *Hawaii Reg.* 19 | 16 | 18 | $32

(aka Breakfast, Lunch & Crab)

Iwilei | 580 N. Nimitz Hwy. (bet. Kukahi & Pacific Sts.) | Honolulu | 808-545-7979 | www.samchoy.com

Expect a "rollicking", "no-frills setting" at this "family-friendly" joint "away from the tourist hangouts" in Iwilei, where the Hawaii Regional fare comes in "huge portions" - bring a "carry-on for leftovers"; the "standout poke" and "gravy-laden loco moco" are the reasons some "love anything Sam", but others leave "uninspired" by the "slow service" and a concept they feel has "jumped the shark."

	FOOD	DECOR	SERVICE	COST

Z Sansei *Japanese/Pacific Rim* 25 | 18 | 22 | $46

Waikiki | Waikiki Beach Marriott Resort & Spa | 2552 Kalakaua Ave. (bet. Ohua & Paoakalani Aves.) | Honolulu | 808-931-6286 | www.sanseihawaii.com

"What a find" exclaim enthusiasts of this "popular" island chainlet where the Japanese and Pacific Rim fare - from "exceptional sushi" to "inventive" seafood and "killer cocktails" - "dazzles the palate"; "plan on a long wait" "even with reservations", as well as "noise" and iffy service at some locales, but you'll be rewarded by "chefs who love their work"; P.S. locals "get in line early" for the "fantastic" early-bird specials, when the place really gets "packed."

Sarento's Top of the "I" *Italian* 19 | 22 | 21 | $53

Waikiki | The Ilikai | 1777 Ala Moana Blvd. (Hobron Ln.) | Honolulu | 808-955-5559 | www.tristarrestaurants.com

The "epic views" of Waikiki are "what you pay for" at this Italian atop the Ilikai Hotel, where the "incomparable" vistas and "considerate staff" make it just right for a "romantic dinner"; but those put off by the "tired interior" and "expensive", "not terribly innovative" fare (did they "corner the market on garlic"?) advise "have an overpriced drink and limit your losses."

Sergio's *Italian* ▽ 18 | 16 | 16 | $46

(aka Sergio's Italian Table)

Waikiki | Hilton Hawaiian Vill., 2nd fl. | 2005 Kalia Rd. (Ala Moana Blvd.) | Honolulu | 808-951-6900 | www.sergioshawaii.net

Across from the main lobby at Waikiki's bustling Hilton Hawaiian Village, this "friendly", second-floor Italian with an ocean view delivers "solid" if "unremarkable" (and somewhat "pricey") fare that's best enjoyed during "early-bird" hours; an "eager-to-please" staff helps.

Shirokiya *Japanese* 21 | 8 | 13 | $14

Ala Moana | Shirokiya, Ala Moana Ctr. | 1450 Ala Moana Blvd. (bet. Atkinson Dr. & Piikoi St.) | Honolulu | 808-973-9111 | www.shirokiya.com

"Cheap", "local-style" Japanese is the name of the game at this "awesome" food court on the upper level of Ala Moana Center's

Shirokiya department store, offering an "incredible selection" of "freshly made" fare including sushi, gyoza, tempura, saimin, bento boxes and other "unique" items; it's a "noisy", kid-filled, "search-for-a-seat" type of place, so regulars recommend doing "the full walk around before making your choice", then "taking it out" "to the beach."

Shokudo ◐ *Japanese* 22 | 21 | 18 | $31

Ala Moana | Ala Moana Pacific Ctr. | 1585 Kapiolani Blvd. (Kaheka St.) | Honolulu | 808-941-3701 | www.shokudojapanese.com

The "bright", "modern" decor and "young crowd" create a "lively atmosphere" that's perfect for "group gatherings" at this warehouse-size Ala Moana izakaya-style eatery; reviewers recommend the "creatively presented" Japanese "with-a-twist" dishes like "wonderful housemade tofu", sushi pizza, shiso fries, mochi au gratin and ice cream-filled toast, but have less enthusiasm for the "slow service."

Shore Bird *American* 16 | 20 | 16 | $30

Waikiki | Outrigger Reef on the Beach | 2169 Kalia Rd. (bet. Beachwalk & Saratoga Rd.) | Honolulu | 808-922-2887 | www.outriggerreef-onthebeach.com

DIY-ers have "a blast" "cooking the meat" "on a gigantic grill" at this "inexpensive" Waikiki American "on the water's edge" at the Outrigger Reef on the Beach; the "fantastic location", generous buffet and "friendly" staff win points, but some find the fare "hit-or-miss", and grouse about their clothes "smelling like smoke"; P.S. you don't have to man the stoves at breakfast or lunch.

Side Street Inn ◐ *American* 24 | 9 | 18 | $27

Ala Moana | 1225 Hopaka St. (bet. Pensacola St. & Piikoi St.) | Honolulu | 808-591-0253

NEW **Kapahulu** | 614 Kapahulu Ave. (Campbell Ave.) | Honolulu | 808-739-3939

www.sidestreetinn.com

Locally known as "a dive with the best pork chops" and fried rice in town, this Ala Moana "real deal" with a "gritty alley entrance" and "well-worn furniture" prides itself on "large quantities" of "family-style" American comfort fare "mixed with local flair" (lilikoi ribs, Big Island smoked pork); while the recently opened second location on

Kapahulu is "more modern", the "local chefs hang out" at the original, where "parking is a nightmare" and the "always busy, but attentive" staff takes a while to warm up to nonregulars.

Singha Thai Cuisine *Thai* 21 | 21 | 21 | $31

Waikiki | Canterbury Pl. | 1910 Ala Moana Blvd. (Ena Rd.) | Honolulu | 808-941-2898 | www.singhathai.com

It's a little "touristy" at this Waikiki Thai, but the "beautiful" setting - "tropical flowers everywhere", walls "covered with silk hangings" and nightly dancers - wins fans; the "reasonably priced" fare is "reliable" (even if some say "the heat's dumbed down") and the staff "knows how to run a restaurant", which is why it's almost "always full."

Sorabol ◐ *Korean* 22 | 12 | 17 | $29

Ala Moana | 805 Keeaumoku St. (Rycroft Blvd.) | Honolulu | 808-947-3113 | www.sorabolhawaii.com

You may "see people drinking beer and soju at 8 AM" with their kimchi at this 24-hour Ala Moana Korean, where the "fast" staff and "highly touted", "not too Americanized" fare (bulgogi, hong chang, kalbi) make up for "absolutely no atmosphere"; there's "nothing unusual or spectacular here" unless you count the "late-night hours."

Spices Ⓜ *Asian* ▽ 24 | 16 | 21 | $25

Moiliili | 2671 S. King St. (Kahuna Ln.) | Honolulu | 808-949-2679 | www.spiceshawaii.com

A "unique blend" of cuisines at this Moiliili Pan-Asian - from Laotian and Thai to Vietnamese and Malaysian - turns up "creative" "dishes not available elsewhere"; while the space, featuring Southeast Asian art and photos, isn't as impressive as the fare, "nice touches" include a wallet-friendly BYO policy.

Stage Ⓢ *American/Asian* 22 | 22 | 21 | $46

(aka Stage Restaurant & Amuse Wine Bar)

Ala Moana | Honolulu Design Ctr. | 1250 Kapiolani Blvd., 2nd fl. (Pensacola St.) | Honolulu | 808-237-5429 | www.stagerestauranthawaii.com

The "striking lighting" and "designer" look of this "pricey" Ala Moana Pan-Asian-New American in the Honolulu Design Center is "fitting for its location" - and so is chef Ron de Guzman's "excellent", modern menu highlighting local ingredients for a "see-and-be-seen" crowd; though a few say service could be "tighter", most "highly recommend it"; P.S. the adjacent Amuse wine bar offers 80 labels by the glass from self-serve carousels.

Suntory *Japanese* 23 | 20 | 22 | $51

Waikiki | Royal Hawaiian Ctr. | 2233 Kalakaua Ave. (bet. Royal Hawaiian & Seaside Aves.) | Honolulu | 808-922-5511 | www.restaurantsuntory.com

Some of "the best teppanyaki in town" is served at this Royal Hawaiian Center Japanese in Waikiki, but, then again, "everything they make is fantastic" - including "classic bento boxes executed perfectly", "authentic" sukiyaki and sushi; though it's on the "pricey" side, the "aesthetic surroundings" and solid service help justify the cost.

Sushi King ◐ *Japanese* 19 | 12 | 16 | $25

Moiliili | 2700 S. King St. (bet. Kahaoloa & Kahuna Lns.) | Honolulu | 808-947-2836

"Go for the lunch specials" or the "excellent" early-bird dinners advise admirers of this "affordable", "local-style" Japanese in Moiliili, where there's "consistent" fare and "oddly interesting" decor; but less-enamored diners are rankled by "rough-around-the-edges" service and "mediocre sushi", labeling it "average all around."

Z Sushi Sasabune ⊠ *Japanese* 28 | 16 | 21 | $87

Ala Moana | 1419 S. King St. (Keeaumoku St.) | Honolulu | 808-947-3800 | www.sasabunehawaii.com

"You can definitely trust" Seiji Kumagawa to prepare an "absolutely amazing" omakase with "melt-in-your-mouth" fish "flown in that day" at this Ala Moana Japanese, voted Hawaii's No. 1 for Food; ok, those put off by "dictatorial" service (the chef "gets mad if you don't eat something") are "not quite comfortable" here, the decor isn't stellar and it may be the "priciest sushi on the island", but fans say it would be hard to find better "anywhere in the world."

Tanaka of Tokyo *Japanese* 21 | 18 | 21 | $42

Ala Moana | Ala Moana Ctr. | 1450 Ala Moana Blvd. (bet. Atkinson Dr. & Piikoi St.) | Honolulu | 808-945-3443

(continued)

Tanaka of Tokyo

Waikiki | King's Vill. | 131 Kaiulani Ave. (bet. Koa Ave. & Price Edward St.) | Honolulu | 808-922-4233
Waikiki | Waikiki Shopping Plaza | 2250 Kalakaua Ave. (bet. Royal Hawaiian & Seaside Aves.) | Honolulu | 808-922-4702
www.tanakaoftokyo.com

You "sit around the grill" meeting "tourists from other countries" at this "busy", teppanyaki-style Japanese trio, where the "talented" chefs provide plenty of "flaming, flying" "entertainment" "for the grandkids"; a handful deem the experience "nothing to write home about", and what's a "good value" to some is "overpriced" to others.

Tangö Contemporary Cafe *American*

24 | 20 | 22 | $33

Downtown | Hokua | 1288 Ala Moana Blvd. (bet. Piikoi & Queen Sts.) | Honolulu | 808-593-7288 | www.tangocafehawaii.com

It's "tough to get a reservation now that the secret is out" at this "reasonably priced" Downtown New American in the Hokua condominium, but the "trendy fare", via chef Göran Streng, is "worth the table space fight"; further pluses include a "helpful staff" and modern decor featuring birch trees and globe pendant lights.

Tanioka's *Japanese/Seafood*

24 | 9 | 19 | $15

(aka Tanioka's Seafoods & Catering)

Waipahu | 94-903 Farrington Hwy. (bet. Awalau & Awamoku Sts.) | 808-671-3779 | www.taniokas.com

With "da best poke", "fish patties to die for" and a "nice selection of prepared foods", this family-owned, okazuya-style Japanese seafood market in a Waipahu strip mall is the spot to "design your own plate lunch to go"; it's counter-service only and there are "long lines at lunchtime", but the "customer-first attitude" and variety of "so much good stuff" mean you "can't stop buying."

Taormina *Italian*

25 | 23 | 23 | $56

Waikiki | 227 Lewers St. (Don Ho Ln.) | Honolulu | 808-926-5050 | www.taorminarestaurant.com

"One of the few Sicilian restaurants on the island", this "casual, yet high-end" Italian in Waikiki proffers a "sophisticated" menu with "favorites" like "sea urchin pasta" and "seafood bruschetta"; the "excellent" staff, "modern" space with patio dining and valet parking enhance this rather "expensive" experience.

Tavola Tavola *Italian* ▽ 22 | 15 | 22 | $43

Diamond Head | 3106 Monsarrat Ave. (Kanaina Ave.) | Honolulu | 808-737-6600 | www.tavolatavola.net

Fans of this Northern Italian "on the slopes of Diamond Head" cite the "unique" dishes focused on the Emilia Romagna region, crafted, somewhat surprisingly, by a Japanese chef; the contemporary, "low-key setting" is "comfortable" for a "quiet, intimate" dinner, though a few complain about "expensive" tabs.

3660 on the Rise Ⓜ *Pacific Rim* 25 | 21 | 24 | $53

Kaimuki | 3660 Waialae Ave. (Wilhelmina Rise) | Honolulu | 808-737-1177 | www.3660.com

The "seafood *no ka oi* [is the best]" at this "Oahu staple for fine dining" in Kaimuki, where chef Russell Siu creates "memorable" Pacific Rim cuisine "with local accents", including his signature ahi katsu, which is complemented by an "excellent" (albeit "pricey") wine list and served by "waiters with plenty of aloha"; while some find the decor "tasteful", others feel it "needs updating" and deem the "difficult-to-find" location a "minus", but fans are glad to be "away from the tourist areas."

Tiki's Grill & Bar ◐ *Pacific Rim* 17 | 20 | 17 | $30

Waikiki | Aston Waikiki Beach Hotel | 2570 Kalakaua Ave., 2nd fl. (bet. Kapahulul & Paoakalani Aves.) | Honolulu | 808-923-8454 | www.tikisgrill.com

"You've gotta love" this hotel tiki bar's "location overlooking Waikiki beach", where the sunsets and "fresh breezes" go perfectly with "awesome" drinks and a "pretty" staff; but those not into the "Polynesian kitsch" contend that it's "blanded itself to pander to tourists" with "so-so" Pacific Rim fare and "slow service."

Tony Roma's *BBQ* 19 | 16 | 18 | $30

Aiea | Westridge Shopping Ctr. | 98-150 Kaonohi St. (bet. Moanalua Loop & Moanalua Rd.) | 808-487-9911

(continued)

Tony Roma's

Waikiki | 1972 Kalakaua Ave. (Pau St.) | Honolulu | 808-942-2121 www.tonyromas.com

There's "always decent BBQ" at the two reasonably priced Oahu outposts of this Miami-bred national chain, where the service is "fast" and what fans call "the best ribs in town" "fall off the bone"; still, dissenters cite a "corporate" atmosphere and "just ok" fare, snapping "you can get this anywhere, try something local."

Town [S] *American/Italian* — 24 | 17 | 20 | $36

Kaimuki | 3435 Waialae Ave. (9th Ave.) | Honolulu | 808-735-5900 | www.townkaimuki.com

"Don't tell anyone about this place, it's already too crowded" plead patrons of this "hip" "locavore nirvana" in Kaimuki, where chef Ed Kenney's "amazing" New American-Italian dishes "emphasize local, organic", sustainable ingredients; the "industrial-minimalist" space gets "noisy" and service "can be inconsistent", but that doesn't keep the "trendy" crowd from wishing it could devour "rich gnocchi" and "melt-in-your-mouth polenta" "every night"; there's counter-service at breakfast and lunch.

Tsukuneya ◐ *Japanese* — ▽ 20 | 19 | 18 | $44

(aka Robata Grill Tsukuneya Style)

University | 1442 University Ave. (Dole St.) | Honolulu | 808-943-0390 | www.tsukuneyarobatagrill.com

The "authentic Japanese" fare at this "oasis in the University area" "accommodates local flair", from "satisfying" homemade tofu, to "oh-so-good" tsukune, kiawe-broiled robata yaki and "great sake"; the comfortable setting is laid-back casual, so the only complaint is the "wish for a better wine list."

12th Ave. Grill [S] *American* — 24 | 18 | 22 | $39

Kaimuki | 1145 12th Ave. (bet. Harding & Waialae Aves.) | Honolulu | 808-732-9469 | www.12thavegrill.com

Aficionados advise it's "good to make a reservation" at this "small", "charming hideaway" in Kaimuki that's "always crowded" thanks to a "varied", "seasonal" menu of "innovative" New American "comfort food" featuring "locally grown produce", complemented by a "super wine list", "attentive but unobtrusive" service and an "unpretentious chic" atmosphere; while some grouse about "cramped" seating, overly "dim" lighting and "noise", many agree this "neighborhood find" is as "good as it gets in the cost-to-value ratio."

21 Degrees North [S] [M] *Seafood* ∇ 21 | 23 | 22 | $57

Kahuku | Turtle Bay Resort | 57-091 Kamehameha Hwy. (Kuilima Dr.) | 808-293-8811 | www.turtlebayresort.com

A "drop-dead setting" with "million-dollar" vistas from Oahu's North Shore is the "big seller" for this "jewel" in Kahuku's Turtle Bay Resort, and "great service" also helps to "make the trip enjoyable"; while fans find the seasonal Pacific Rim fare featuring "fresh fish" "enjoyable", many say that the "view outdoes the quality of the food."

Uncle's Fish Market *Seafood* 21 | 15 | 16 | $23

Iwilei | 1135 N. Nimitz Hwy. (Pier 38) | Honolulu | 808-275-0063 | www.unclesfishmarket.com

The "fishing paraphernalia" hanging on the walls "looks authentic" at this "unpretentious" pierside seafooder in Iwilei that serves fin fare "right off the docks" coupled with "cold beer" and "live music" on weekends; those who find the area a bit of a "ghost town" after dark, however, complain it's "costly for what you get and where you are" so "go for lunch" instead.

Verbano Italiano *Italian* 19 | 16 | 21 | $29

Kaimuki | 1126 Koko Head Ave. (Mahina Ave.) | Honolulu | 808-735-1777
Waikiki | 1451 S. King St. (bet. Kaheka & Keeaumoku Sts.) | Honolulu | 808-941-9168

Verbano Pastaria *Italian*

Aiea | Pearlridge Ctr. E. | 98-151 Pali Momi St. (Kamehameha Hwy.) | 808-487-1118

www.verbanohawaii.com

The "consistent" Italian fare, "friendly service" and "reasonable prices" make this trio of Oahu Sicilians a "casual neighborhood choice" for "last-minute" meals; the dishes may not be inventive, and the "small" quarters bother some, but with an "extensive menu" that includes all the "standards", they work for families and groups.

	FOOD	DECOR	SERVICE	COST

Vietnam Café Pho Saigon *Vietnamese* ∇ 25 | 13 | 19 | $24

Chinatown | 52 N. Hotel St. (Smith St.) | Honolulu | 808-536-8462

For "cheap, fast" and "consistent" pho served by an "attentive" staff, the "aloha-shirt business crowd" "slurp, slurp, slurps" at this casual Vietnamese standby in Chinatown; expect "lots" of "unique", "hot and spicy finds", but not much in the way of decor.

Vino Italian Tapas & Wine Bar S M *Italian* 24 | 22 | 24 | $40
(aka Vino)

Restaurant Row | 500 Ala Moana Blvd. (bet. Punchbowl & South Sts.) | Honolulu | 808-524-8466 | www.dkrestaurants.com

Oenophiles have "gotta go" to D.K. Kodama's "fantastic" Restaurant Row wine bar "at least once" insist fans of "knowledgeable" master sommelier Chuck Furuya, who's "always there" and "happy to suggest" a "boutique wine" for pairing (or "ask for ones not on the list", since there's a larger stash in back); the "amazing", "ever-changing" Italian tapas menu is "varied" enough for most, plus the "friendly" setting encourages lingering.

Wahoo's Fish Taco *Mexican* 18 | 12 | 14 | $14

Ward | Ward Gateway Ctr. | 940 Auahi St. (Ward Ave.) | Honolulu | 808-591-1646 | www.wahooshawaii.com

"These dudes know how to make a fish taco" hail admirers of this Ward Gateway "fast-fooder" by way of California that offers a "huge variety" of "cheap" Mexican fare; those who "return time and time again" "love" the "enormous burritos", breadth of choices and "cheerful" counter service, but others bypass it, citing a "stereotypical surfer" setting, "ridiculously loud music" and "nothing-special" "quick bites."

Wild Ginger Asian *Asian* ∇ 21 | 16 | 20 | $29

Kaimuki | 3441 Waialae Ave. (9th Ave.) | Honolulu | 808-738-1168

The "interesting variety" of Pan-Asian dishes - from Thai to Malaysian to Chinese - at this Kaimuki neighborhood spot has such "mouthwatering sauces" that some diners "want to pick up the plate and drink"; there's "attentive service" and reasonable prices as well, but you'll have to look past the "nothing-special decor."

Willows, The *American/Hawaiian* 18 | 22 | 17 | $36

Moiliili | 901 Hausten St. (S. King St.) | Honolulu | 808-952-9200 | www.willowshawaii.com

The "garden location is a plus" - and probably the high point - of this "old-time" Moiliili American with plenty of "local Hawaiian fare" in its outdoor, "all-you-can-eat", "bargain" buffet; it's a "go-to place" "for local family gatherings" with just the right "unhurried service", though detractors deem it a "kitschy" choice with "average" eats.

Wolfgang's Steakhouse *Steak* 24 | 23 | 23 | $68

Waikiki | Royal Hawaiian Ctr. | 2301 Kalakaua Ave., 3rd fl. (bet. Duke's Ln. & Seaside Ave.) | Honolulu | 808-922-3600 | www.wolfgangssteakhouse.net

An offshoot of its NYC and Beverly Hills siblings, this "consummate" steakhouse in Waikiki's Royal Hawaiian Center has all the trappings of a "special-occasion" spot: "over-the-top service", "juicy, premium-quality beef sizzling in butter", "hefty sides", an "elegant" open-air space and "expensive" tabs; it's just a "disappointed" few who find "there's better" meat meccas in town; P.S. "fantastic" happy hours offer "cheap drinks" and bites at the bar.

Yanagi Sushi ◐ *Japanese* 23 | 15 | 20 | $44

Kakaako | 762 Kapiolani Blvd. (Cooke St.) | Honolulu | 808-597-1525 | www.yanagisushi-hawaii.com

"Reasonably priced", "excellent sushi", "ahi to die for" and the "lightest shrimp tempura" are the reasons it's "always crowded" at this Kakaako Japanese veteran that's even better if "you're up and hungry after 10 PM" when the "late-night specials" kick in; though sticklers snipe "time has not been kind" to this "worn" spot, others appreciate "walls covered with celebrity photos" as well as "friendly chefs."

Yohei Sushi ⊠ *Japanese* 25 | 16 | 22 | $41

Kapalama | 1111 Dillingham Blvd. (Kokea St.) | Honolulu | 808-841-3773

"Sit at the sushi bar and let the chef amaze you" say fans of this Kapalama Japanese that's "popular with locals and nationals" for its "fresh", "artistically" presented seafood and "excellent" *teishoku*; the staff of "old-timers" "treats you like family", but tables "right next to each other" make the space feel "cramped."

FOOD | DECOR | SERVICE | COST

Maui

TOP FOOD

27 Mama's Fish | *Seafood*
Hali'imaile Gen. | *Hawaii Reg.*
26 Spago | *Californian/Pacific Rim*
Gerard's | *French*
Merriman's | *Hawaii Reg.*

TOP DECOR

27 Spago
Son'z/Swan Court
Mama's Fish
Feast at Lele
26 Humuhumunukunukuapua'a

TOP SERVICE

26 Gerard's
Spago
Son'z/Swan Court
25 Lahaina Grill
Banyan Tree

BEST BUYS

1. Aloha Mixed Plate
2. Gazebo
3. Cilantro Grill
4. Maui Tacos
5. Kihei Caffe

Aloha Mixed Plate *Hawaiian* — 21 | 17 | 19 | $16

Lahaina | 1285 Front St. (Kapunakea St.) | 808-661-3322 | www.alohamixedplate.com

An "unmatched location" with "spectacular" views and "luau music" next door sets the stage for "terrific plate lunches" of "*ono*" "Hawaiian favorites" at this "authentic" Lahaina "gem", where "huge portions" at "no-frills prices" equals "excellent value"; some fret that the "friendly" staff appears "overworked", and while the decor may be "patio plastic", "who cares when you front the crystal-blue Pacific?"

Aroma D'Italia *Italian* — ∇ 19 | 15 | 20 | $30

Kihei | Kihei Town Ctr. | 1881 S. Kihei Rd. (Halelani Pl.) | 808-879-0133 | www.aromaditaliamaui.com

For "family-priced dining" fans head to this "neighborhood Italian" in Kihei serving Sicilian fare with that "Sunday-at-grandma's taste"; while some grouse that the strip-mall space is "not much on atmosphere", "attentive", "child-friendly" service helps make it a "pleasant" experience and a "good value."

A Saigon Café *Vietnamese* — 23 | 11 | 21 | $25

Wailuku | 1792 Main St. (Kaniela St.) | 808-243-9560

Even though it now sports a "new sign", this Wailuku "hole-in-the-wall" is still "difficult to find" for non-"locals", but "well worth the effort" for "authentic", "tantalizing" Vietnamese fare full of "exciting flavors", served by "chatty", "entertaining" waiters who seem to be "rehearsing for Comedy Central"; the "1950s cafeteria decor" is largely "irrelevant" to phonatics who "always leave feeling that it's money well spent."

Banyan Tree [S] [M] *Eclectic* 24 | 26 | 25 | $62

Kapalua | Ritz-Carlton Kapalua | 1 Ritz-Carlton Dr. (Office Rd.) | 808-669-6200 | www.ritzcarlton.com

When you feel like "putting on the Ritz, Hawaiian-style", "nothing could be finer" than the "beautiful" room with "incredible views" of "sunsets over the sea" and service that "makes you feel like a rock star" at the Ritz-Carlton Kapalua's "first-rate" signature restaurant offering "exceptional" Eclectic cuisine; it's a "memorable dining experience" and, not surprisingly, an "expensive" one, though "half-price wine bottles" on Wednesday nights help lighten the tabs.

Bubba Gump Shrimp Co. *American/Seafood* 16 | 18 | 18 | $28

Lahaina | 889 Front St. (Papalaua St.) | 808-661-3111 | www.bubbagump.com

See review in Oahu Directory.

Buzz's Wharf *Seafood/Steak* 20 | 17 | 19 | $35

Maalaea | Maalaea Bay Harbor (off Hwy. 30) | 808-244-5426 | www.buzzswharf.com

A "spectacular view" of Maalaea Bay Harbor is the highlight of this "reliable" harborside eatery serving "reasonably priced" surf 'n' turf "staples", as well as "amazing" Tahitian prawns and other "fantastic" shrimp dishes; though some say it looks every bit the "fish house from the '60s" that it is and contend that service "could be better", most agree it's a "good value" for a "family meal."

Cafe O'Lei *Seafood/Steak* 24 | 19 | 22 | $33

Kahului | The Dunes at Maui Laui | 1333 Maui Lani Pkwy. (Hoomoku St.) | 808-877-0073

Kihei | Rainbow Mall | 2439 S. Kihei Rd. (bet. Alanui Ke Alii Rd. & Keonekai St.) | 808-891-1368 [M]

NEW **Napili** | Outrigger Napili Shores | 5315 Lower Honoapiilani Rd. (Hui Rd.) | 808-442-3633 [S] [M]

(continued)

Cafe O'Lei

NEW **Wailuku** | 200 Halewaiu Rd. (Kahekili Rd.) | 808-242-2770
Wailuku | Pono Ctr. | 62 N. Market St. (bet. Hwy. 32 & Vineyard St.) | 808-986-0044 ☒
www.cafeoleirestaurants.com

There's "more gourmet than meets the eye" at this Hawaiian chain offering "creative dining at a reasonable cost", including "excellent", "fresh" local seafood, "wonderful" steaks and "colorful, inventive cocktails", in a "casual" setting where "foodies and surfers can mingle"; "friendly, prompt" service and "convenient locations" make them "family favorites", and though the eldest sibling in Kihei occupies an "uninspiring strip-mall locale", the "food and prices more than make up for it."

NEW California Pizza Kitchen *Pizza* 20 | 17 | 19 | $24

Kahului | Kahului International Airport | 1 Kahului Airport Rd. (Keolani Pl.) | 808-877-5858 | www.cpk.com

See review in Oahu Directory.

NEW Cane & Taro *Hawaiian* 19 | 20 | 20 | $35

Kaanapali | Whaler's Vill. | 2435 Kaanapali Pkwy. (off Honoapiilani Hwy.) | 808-662-0668 | www.dkrestaurants.com

You "can't beat the location" of this newest eatery from Sansei's D.K. Kodama, a "nice addition to Whaler's Village" in Kaanapali, where a "helpful, friendly" staff serves "unique breakfasts, lunches and dinners" of Hawaiian fare featuring "locally grown products" in a "lovely" setting with "beautiful views of sunsets"; "great early-bird specials" are another plus, though some feel "everything is ok, but nothing is exceptional" on a menu that "tries to do too much."

Capische? *Italian* 25 | 25 | 24 | $65

Wailea | Hotel Wailea | 555 Kaukahi St. (Kalai Waa Dr.) | 808-879-2224 | www.capische.com

For a "breath of fresh air" – literally – fans head to the Hotel Wailea's Northern Italian, which offers "beautiful alfresco dining" with views of "awe-inspiring sunsets" from its hillside location "perched high above the Pacific", plus "inventive", "exquisite" Italian cuisine, including "wonderful" nightly specials; service comes "with lots of aloha" ("almost too friendly" for some), and while it's "pricey and out of the way", devotees tout it a "great place for a special occasion - like any day that ends in 'y.'"

Casanova *Italian* 20 | 16 | 19 | $33

Makawao | 1188 Makawao Ave. (Baldwin Ave.) | 808-572-0220

NEW **Bistro Casanova** ☒ *Italian*

Kahului | 33 Lono Ave. (Kaahumanu Ave.) | 808-873-3650
www.casanovamaui.com

Some of the "best eats Upcountry" can be found at this Makawao "institution" offering "classic, solid Italian fare" at "value prices" in a "family-friendly" setting, where service from the "young, tanned" staff "reflects the laid-back Maui lifestyle", and things get "noisy" "when the dance floor becomes a disco with DJ"; its newer sibling in Downtown Kahului offers a Med-Northern Italian menu, including tapas, in a stylish Euro setting with patio seating.

Castaway Café *Continental* 21 | 18 | 23 | $28

Kaanapali | Aston Maui Kaanapali Villas | 45 Kai Ala Dr. (Honoapiilani Hwy.) | 808-661-9091 | www.castawaycafe.com

Still a "secret with visitors", this "kid-friendly" Continental at the Aston Maui Kaanapali Villas is "where locals go" for "excellent" breakfasts, casual dinners fueled by a "knockout wine list at great price points" and "super-nice" service in an "island-friendly atmosphere"; while most regard the interior as "very ordinary", the "beachside" view is "extraordinary."

Charley's *American* 22 | 15 | 21 | $24

Paia | 142 Hana Hwy. (Baldwin Ave.) | 808-579-9453 | www.charleysmaui.com

This Paia American is a "tradition after sunrise" for many "hippies, cowboys and surfers" (and occasionally "Willie Nelson"), who come for one of the "best breakfasts on Maui", including mac-nut pancakes ("heaven wrapped in coconut syrup"), as well as "phenomenal" pizzas and other "down-home" eats; cynics describe the scene as "aging everything - including the clientele", but the crowds who keep it "packed every night" don't seem to mind.

	FOOD	DECOR	SERVICE	COST

Cheeseburger in Paradise *American* 17 | 18 | 17 | $22

Lahaina | 811 Front St. (Lahainaluna Rd.) | 808-661-4855

Cheeseburger Island Style *American*

Kihei | The Shops at Wailea | 3750 Waila Alanui Dr. (Wailea Ike Dr.) | 808-874-8990

www.cheeseburgerland.com

See review in Oahu Directory.

Cilantro Grill *Mexican* 23 | 14 | 18 | $17

Lahaina | Old Lahaina Ctr. | 170 Papalaua Ave. (bet. Front & Wainee Sts.) | 808-667-5444 | www.cilantrogrill.com

Though it's "quick" and "cheap", the Mexican fare at this Lahaina BYO is "not fast food" assert aficionados, but rather "fresh", "addictive" eats that "earn praise from even the most persnickety palates", served by a "staff that cares"; the mood is "cheerful" in the "casual" setting with "nice high ceilings and pleasing colors", but even so some prefer to get it "to go."

Colleen's at the Cannery *American* ∇ 21 | 15 | 19 | $28

Haiku | Haiku Cannery Mktpl. | 810 Haiku Rd. (Kokomo Rd.) | 808-575-9211 | www.colleensinhaiku.com

For "down-home cooking at an Upcountry neighborhood joint", those in the know head to this Haiku New American where the "breakfasts rock" and it's "not bad for dinner", either, offering an all-day menu of dishes featuring local organic ingredients; you can "have a conversation with your dinner partner" in the simple, bistro setting where "most of the diners know each other", and while the service is "not perfect", it's "good" enough.

David Paul's Island Grill *Hawaiian* 26 | 24 | 25 | $57

Lahaina | Lahaina Ctr. | 900 Front St. (bet. Baker & Papalaua Sts.) | 808-662-3000 | www.davidpaulsislandgrill.com

"Welcome back" David Paul Johnson - and "never leave us again" exclaim fans of his Lahaina Hawaiian where an "awesome menu" of "sophisticated", "exquisitely prepared island cuisine", featuring "farm-fresh ingredients", is complemented by "wonderful" cocktails and an "interesting wine list"; the staff is "on top of things" while the "masterful" chef frequently "graces the tables" in the "beautiful" space, with the "Pacific adding its charms and sounds just across the street"; one caveat: it's "not for the faint of wallet."

Dollie's Pub & Café ◐ *Pub Food* ∇ 19 | 12 | 18 | $18

Lahaina | Kahana Manor Shops | 4310 Lower Honoapiilani Rd. (bet. Hoohui Rd. & Piina Pl.) | 808-669-0266 | www.dolliespizzakahana.com

"Get a drink, kick back and chill" at this Lahaina "sports bar" that also serves "very good" pizzas as well as American pub grub staples; critics find the fare "just average" and the service "lackadaisical", while lambasting the "college-age" scene "later in the evening" with "rowdy twentysomethings getting plastered", which may be why some are thankful "takeout" is an option.

Dragon Dragon *Chinese* ∇ 19 | 16 | 17 | $24

Kahului | Maui Mall | 70 E. Kaahumanu Ave. (Hana Hwy.) | 808-893-1628

Sinophiles who feel they "don't have much to choose from for Chinese" on Maui consider this Kahului spot "better than most" for its "traditional" offerings served "with great efficiency" in "clean, bright" surroundings; skeptics find the fare "just ok" and the decor "dated", and wish the staff could "smile a little more."

NEW **Duke's Beach House** *Pacific Rim* 21 | 24 | 21 | $37

Kaanapali | Honua Kai Resort & Spa | 130 Kai Malina Pkwy. (bet. Hwy. 30 & Lower Honoapiilani Rd.) | 808-662-2900 | www.dukesmaui.com

For a "one-of-a-kind Hawaiian experience", fans tout this newest Pacific Rim sibling of Duke's in Waikiki and Kauai, located in a "great spot overlooking the Pacific" at Kaanapali's Honua Kai Resort & Spa, where the "kitschy" surf-themed open-air setting makes you feel like you're in a "beach blanket movie"; "fresh, tasty" seafood and other "innovative island delights" come at "reasonable prices" via "smooth" service; P.S. "save room for the hula pie" dessert.

Duo *Seafood/Steak* 25 | 26 | 25 | $71

Wailea | Four Seasons Resort Maui at Wailea | 3900 Wailea Alanui Dr. (Wailea Ike Dr.) | 808-874-8000 | www.fourseasons.com/maui

Fans call this Four Seasons surf 'n' turf specialist a "must-go if you're staying in Wailea" for its "incredible cuts of beef", "super-fresh seafood" and "locally sourced sides", as well as "impeccable" service in a "poolfront" setting with "can't-beat" views that "make the prices easier to swallow"; while it's an "elegant" option for a "romantic, candlelit dinner", it also serves an "amazing" breakfast buffet.

Feast at Lele *Polynesian* 23 | 27 | 24 | $95

Lahaina | 505 Front St. (Shaw St.) | 808-667-5353 | www.feastatlele.com

"Not your traditional luau, but much better", this "sophisticated experience" in Lahaina is "excellent in every aspect" - a "beautiful beachside" backdrop with the "sun setting" and the occasional "whale breaching", a "spectacular" show of music and dance from the "four different island areas" of Polynesia, "delicious" Polynesian "small courses" and "plentiful" drinks "served at your table" (instead of the usual buffet) by "young, surf-toned", "eager-to-please" staffers; some find it "a little pricey", but many insist "you won't regret it."

Ferraro's *Italian* 24 | 26 | 25 | $65

(aka Ferraro's Bar e Ristorante)

Wailea | Four Seasons Resort Maui at Wailea | 3900 Wailea Alanui Dr. (Wailea Ike Dr.) | 808-874-8000 | www.fourseasons.com/maui

Fans tout this "upscale" "Italian oasis" at the Four Seasons Wailea as a "place to go for special occasions" or when "you want to impress" thanks to its "beautiful" oceanfront setting and "view that can't be beat", generally "superb" service, "fabulous" cuisine and an "outstanding wine list"; the "sounds of ocean waves" and strains of live "classical music" add to the "romantic" ambiance, making for a "memorable experience" - just "make sure the wallet is full before you go."

Five Palms Beach Grill *Pacific Rim/Seafood* 21 | 24 | 21 | $38

Kihei | Mana Kai Resort | 2960 S. Kihei Rd. (bet. Ala Koa St. & Kilohana Dr.) | 808-879-2607 | www.fivepalmsrestaurant.com

For many, it's all about the "fabulous oceanfront location" of this Kihei Pacific Rim seafooder where the "view at sunset is amazing" and the sound of "ocean waves" serves as the "dinner music"; the "well-trained" staff provides "attentive" service and helps foster a "civilized atmosphere", but doubters deem the fare "good but not great" and a "little expensive for what you get", which is why some skip dinner in favor of the "awesome" happy-hour or "well-priced" breakfast menus.

Flatbread Company *Pizza* 25 | 18 | 21 | $23

Paia | 89 Hana Hwy. (Baldwin Ave.) | 808-579-8989 | www.flatbreadcompany.com

Seemingly at home in "hippietown Paia", this local link of the New England-based pizzeria chain dishes out "artfully prepared", "oh-so-good" wood-fired pies featuring "phenomenal" thin crusts topped with "incredibly fresh ingredients" from "local organic farms"; "awesome" salads and a "nice selection of local brews" are also served in the "cozy, rustic" setting with a "surfer" vibe that may account for the "slow" pace of service.

Gannon's - A Pacific View Restaurant *Hawaii Reg.* 23 | 24 | 23 | $51

Wailea | Wailea Golf Course | 100 Wailea Golf Club Dr. (Wailea Alanui Dr.) | 808-875-8080 | www.gannonsrestaurant.com

Chef Bev Gannon (Upcountry's Hali'imaile General Store, Joe's Bar & Grill in Wailea) turned the old Seawatch in Wailea into a "class act" blessed with a "spectacular" location that offers "mesmerizing views" of the ocean and Emerald Golf Course; her "creative" Hawaii Regional cuisine is served by a "friendly, professional" staff, and while some feel it's "still working out the kinks", to others it's a "special treat" "when you're feeling flush."

Gazebo, The *American* 24 | 19 | 23 | $19

Napili | Outrigger Napili Shores | 5315 Lower Honoapiilani Rd. (Hui Rd.) | 808-669-5621

Watching "turtles in tide pools" or "whales offshore" in the "beautiful" Pacific helps make the "long waits" bearable at this American "treasure" in Napili offering "amazing" morning and lunch fare ("incredible pancakes", "impressive omelets"), served "fast" by "some of the nicest waitresses anyplace"; it's "tucked behind a condo complex" so it's "not easy to find", and even with the view, the lines can be "exasperating", but most agree it's "worth it" for "breakfast in heaven."

Genki Sushi *Japanese* 16 | 13 | 16 | $22

Kahului | Maui Mall | 70 E. Kaahumanu Ave. (Hana Hwy.) | 808-873-7776
Lahaina | Lahaina Gateway Ctr. | 435 Keawe St. (Honoapiilani Hwy.) | 808-661-0333
www.genkisushiusa.com
See review in Oahu Directory.

Z Gerard's *French* 26 | 25 | 26 | $67

Lahaina | The Plantation Inn | 174 Lahainaluna Rd. (bet. Luakini & Wainee Sts.) | 808-661-8939 | www.gerardsmaui.com

At Gerard Reversade's Lahaina French, "professionals who love their craft" provide "impeccable" service (rated No. 1 on Maui) "from the moment you enter", and the "experience only gets better", with "delectable" cuisine that "uses many local ingredients" and a "superb wine list" served in a "plantation-house setting" that's "stunning" "despite the lack of an ocean view"; it's the "best place for a splurge" – "if you can afford to go there without wincing" at the check.

Z Hali'imaile General Store *Hawaii Reg.* 27 | 23 | 25 | $50

Makawao | 900 Haliimaile Rd. (Makomako St.) | 808-572-2666 | www.bevgannonrestaurants.com

Bev Gannon's "out-of-the-way destination restaurant" is "worth the drive through the sugar fields" to Hali'imaile for her "phenomenal" Hawaii Regional fare "featuring local, organic ingredients", which is served by an "accommodating" staff in a "charming", "plantation" setting with a "warm", "welcoming" atmosphere; while some caution that there are "no general-store prices" here, for most it's a "delightful experience in every way."

Hard Rock Cafe *American* 15 | 20 | 17 | $28

Lahaina | Lahaina Ctr. | 900 Front St. (bet. Baker & Papalaua Sts.) | 808-667-7400 | www.hardrock.com
See review in Oahu Directory.

Hula Grill *Pacific Rim* 21 | 23 | 21 | $36

Kaanapali | Whalers Vill., Bldg. P | 2435 Kaanapali Pkwy. (off Honoapiilani Hwy.) | 808-667-6636 | www.hulagrill.com
See review in Oahu Directory.

Humuhumunukunukuapua'a *Pacific Rim* 22 | 26 | 22 | $63
(aka Humu Humu)

Wailea | Grand Wailea Resort | 3850 Wailea Alanui Dr. (bet. Kaukahi St. & Wailea Ike Dr.) | 808-875-1234 | www.wailearesortdining.com

"You feel like you're floating on top of a lagoon" at the Grand Wailea Resort's "upscale" Pacific Rim establishment, situated in an open-air, thatched-roof edifice built over a pond with fish that "swim underneath you" as you tuck into their "swimmingly fresh", less fortunate brethren; "wonderful" sunset views are another plus, and new chef Isaac Bancaco "has really improved the menu" (his "Kobe short ribs alone are worth a trip"), and though some critics label it "overpriced" and "touristy", devotees insist it's a "must when you're in Maui."

I'O *Asian* 25 | 23 | 23 | $57

Lahaina | 505 Front St. (Shaw St.) | 808-661-8422 | www.iomaui.com

At this sibling of nearby Pacific'O in Lahaina, a "wonderful blend of all the Pacific islands" is captured in the "creative" Pan-Asian cuisine, which features "wild-caught fish" and the "freshest", "locally grown" produce; the service is "attentive and informative", you can take in "breathtaking, unobstructed ocean views" from both indoors and outdoors, and the "music from the luau next door" can be "either fun or distracting, depending on your mood."

Isana *Korean* ▽ 27 | 21 | 23 | $31

Kihei | 515 S. Kihei Rd. (bet. Kaonoulu St. & Ohukai Rd.) | 808-874-5700 | www.isanarestaurant.net

The "hard-working" owners of this Kihei Korean "take pride" in the "wonderful" BBQ that you grill "at your table", traditional offerings such as bibimbop and "very good" sushi; "dedicated" service and an "unpretentious" vibe add to its allure, and "sunset views are a bonus."

Joe's Bar & Grill *American* 21 | 18 | 21 | $48

Wailea | 131 Wailea Ike Pl. (Wailea Ike Dr.) | 808-875-7767 | www.bevgannonrestaurants.com

"Well-prepared" New American "comfort food" (including "outstanding" seafood) is served by a "friendly" staff at this "casual" eatery overlooking the Wailea Tennis Club from celeb chef Bev Gannon

(Gannon's, Hali'imaile General Store) and husband Joe; though some gripe about "high" prices, "dated" decor and the sounds of "tennis matches" reverberating through the open-air space, the "fabulous sunset view" compensates for many faults.

Kihei Caffe ⊄ *American* 25 | 11 | 19 | $18

Kihei | 1945 S. Kihei Rd. (bet. Alahele & Keala Pls.) | 808-879-2230 | www.kiheicaffe.com

For morning "bliss", aficionados head to this "semi-secret local favorite" in Kihei, a "great alternative to $50 hotel breakfasts" with its "fantastic" omelets and other "fast, hot and delicious" American eats; you "stand in a queue and order at the counter" manned by a "friendly" crew, then "find a seat outside" by the "roadside" - sure, it's "nothing much to look at", but to many it's a "better value than most."

Kimo's *American/Seafood* 21 | 22 | 21 | $40

Lahaina | 845 Front St. (Lahainaluna Rd.) | 808-661-4811 | www.kimosmaui.com

An "oceanfront, open-air dining room" with "spectacular" views and "romantic" sunsets, "fresh" seafood "prepared several ways", "amazing mai tais" and "friendly" service - this Lahaina "classic" is just about "what you'd expect your Hawaiian experience to be"; "non-fussy", "reasonably priced" American staples, such as prime rib, are "tasty", "if not particularly inspired", and while a few dismiss it as a "tourist trap", to regulars it's as "comfortable and familiar as a nice old beach flip-flop"; P.S. "save room for the hula pie."

Kobe Japanese Steak House & Oku's Sushi Bar ◐ *Japanese* 22 | 18 | 21 | $42

Lahaina | 136 Dickenson St. (Luakini St.) | 808-667-5555 | www.kobemaui.com

See review in Oahu Directory.

Kula Lodge & Restaurant *American* 21 | 21 | 21 | $32

Kula | 15200 Haleakala Hwy. (bet. Ainakula Rd. & Upper Kimo Dr.) | 808-878-1535 | www.kulalodge.com

The "yummy breakfasts" at this Kula American "warm the soul" - especially "after freezing while watching the sunrise on

Haleakala" - and the pizzas baked in an "outdoor oven" are "phenomenal", but for most, the "breathtaking" mountain views are the main attraction; while a few feel the "wood-paneled old lodge" "could stand a little remodel", many appreciate the "comfortable chairs" as they "recover from the altitude", not to mention the "friendly, efficient" service.

Lahaina Coolers ◐ *Eclectic* 19 | 16 | 20 | $26

Lahaina | 180 Dickenson St. (Wainee St.) | 808-661-7082 | www.lahainacoolers.net

A "hidden gem for late-night food" "off the main drag" in Lahaina, this Eclectic serves three meals a day, including "awesome breakfasts", at "decent prices", plus a "sneakily cheap cocktail menu"; run by some of the "nicest people" around, it has a "laid-back, easygoing" vibe, and while it's "more of a locals' place", "visitors are welcome too."

Lahaina Grill *American* 26 | 24 | 25 | $62

Lahaina | Lahaina Inn | 127 Lahainaluna Rd. (Front St.) | 808-667-5117 | www.lahainagrill.com

Fans report that "David Paul may have moved, but the quality is still here" at this Lahaina New American where the "ingenious" fare and "excellent" wine list "never disappoint", and the "approachable" staff provides "outstanding" service; though it "lacks that million-dollar view", the "sophisticated" space graced with "lots of artwork" is "warm and inviting", and while some find the prices "outrageous", most agree the "upscale" experience is "something to remember."

Leilani's on the Beach *Seafood/Steak* 20 | 22 | 21 | $37

Kaanapali | Whalers Vill., Bldg. J | 2435 Kaanapali Pkwy. (off Honoapiilani Hwy.) | 808-661-4495 | www.leilanis.com

The "fantastic sunset views" are "so-o romantic" at this open-air surf 'n' turf specialist on Kaanapali Beach, where "whales-a-jumpin'" in winter and "people-watching on the beachfront walk" are added attractions; "delightful" service, a "family-friendly" atmosphere and "mai tais to die for" complement the "dependable", "well-prepared" fare.

	FOOD	DECOR	SERVICE	COST

Longhi's *Italian* 21 | 20 | 20 | $44

Lahaina | 888 Front St. (Papalaua St.) | 808-667-2288
Wailea | Shops at Wailea | 3750 Wailea Alanui Dr. (Wailea Ike Dr.) | 808-891-8883
www.longhis.com

"Fabulous" breakfasts are the hallmark of this "classy" Italian chain that also offers a "diverse menu" of "consistent" "red-sauce" and seafood offerings served by a "friendly", "knowledgeable" staff; the open-air Lahaina original offers a "spectacular view" of the ocean, though some insist Wailea is "much better for ambiance and decor", while shoppers swear the "terrace is a must for a day at Ala Moana"; still, a contingent of critics cite "average food" at "steep prices" and "indifferent" service, concluding that it's "lost its touch."

Makawao Steak House *Steak* ∇ 20 | 20 | 20 | $49

Makawao | 3612 Baldwin Ave. (Brewer Rd.) | 808-572-8711

You feel like you're at a "dude ranch" at Makawao's "hometown steakhouse" offering lots of "local" color (think "wagon-wheel chandeliers") and the "meat to match", plus an "excellent salad bar"; the old-school setting "feels like a 1950s restaurant", but the "friendly" service never gets old; P.S. it also serves afternoon tea Wednesdays-Saturdays.

Mala Ocean Tavern *Hawaii Reg./Seafood* 25 | 20 | 22 | $45
(aka Mala)

Lahaina | 1307 Front St. (Kapunakea St.) | 808-667-9394 | www.malaoceantavern.com

Mala Wailea *Hawaii Reg./Seafood*

Wailea | Marriott Wailea Beach Resort & Spa | 3700 Wailea Alanui Dr. (Wailea Ike Dr.) | 808-875-9394 | www.malawailea.com

"Perfectly prepared" seafood highlights the lineup of Mark Ellman's "outstanding, highly creative" Hawaii Regional cuisine that's served by a "friendly, attentive" staff at these Maui twins, which both offer "beautiful views" from their "charming oceanfront locations"; "turtles greet you" at the Lahaina original where "you'll need a scuba tank if you get any closer to the ocean", while many say the Wailea sibling is "much better than you'd expect at a Marriott."

Z Mama's Fish House *Seafood*

27 | 27 | 25 | $64

Paia | 799 Poho Pl. (Hwy. 36) | 808-579-8488 | www.mamasfishhouse.com

This "Maui classic" - voted the island's Most Popular and No. 1 for Food - is "why you come to Hawaii" aver admirers, citing "spectacular", "fresh", "Pan-Pacific" seafood from local waters (the "menu identifies the fishermen who caught your dinner") and "potent drinks", served in a converted "shack" "on a beautiful beach" in Paia before a "palm tree-lined bay"; "excellent, caring" service rounds out the "total package", and while some howl at being on the hook for "outrageous" tabs, most regard it as a "can't-miss destination" that's "worth every penny."

Market Fresh Bistro *Mediterranean*

- | - | - | M

Makawao | The Courtyard | 3620 Baldwin Ave. (Nakui St.) | 808-572-4877

Chef Justin Pardo "rocks" at this Mediterranean bistro tucked away in a small courtyard in a tiny Makawao shopping area, creating "incredible" dishes featuring local ingredients, including seven-course themed tasting dinners twice a month and "super" Sunday brunches that include live ukulele music, which are served in shabby-chic digs that evoke a country kitchen; it's now licensed to serve beer and wine.

Matteo's *Italian*

21 | 17 | 19 | $35

Wailea | 100 Wailea Ike Dr. (Wailea Alanui Dr.) | 808-874-1234 | www.matteosmaui.com

A "reasonable alternative to the high-priced restaurants" in town, this Italian serves up "fantastic" pizzas and "housemade pastas" in a "comfortable", open-air dining room with views of the adjacent Wailea Blue Golf Course; it's "semi-counter service", as "you order up front" and the "friendly" staff brings your food to your table, and while a few shrug that it's "just ok", many value it as an "easy", "cost-effective" place "to take the family for a casual dinner."

Maui Tacos *Mexican*

19 | 8 | 14 | $13

Kahului | Queen Kaahumanu Ctr. | 275 W. Kaahumanu Ave. (S. Wakea Ave.) | 808-871-7726

Kihei | Kamaole Beach Ctr. | 2411 S. Kihei Rd. (Alanui Ke Alii Rd.) | 808-879-5005

(continued)

Maui Tacos

Kihei | Piilani Village Shopping Ctr. | 247 Piikea Ave. (Liloa Dr.) | 808-875-9340
Lahaina | Lahaina Square Shopping Ctr. | 840 Wainee St. (Lahainaluna Rd.) | 808-661-8883
Napili | Napili Plaza | 5095 Napilihau St. (Honoapiilani Hwy.) | 808-665-0222
www.mauitacos.com

"Cultural exchange never tasted so good" as the fish tacos made "with fresh local" fin fare and other Mexican eats with a "Hawaiian slant" at this statewide chain that also boasts an "extensive" salsa bar; "feel-good" prices make it a "great value" and service is "quick" if "minimal", and though there may be "nothing memorable" about the "plastic" surroundings, most prefer to take their "order to-go and drive to the beach", anyway.

Z Merriman's *Hawaii Reg.* 26 | 24 | 25 | $60

Kapalua | Kapalua Resort | 1 Bay Dr. (Bay Rd.) | 808-669-6400 | www.merrimanshawaii.com

See review in Big Island Directory.

Milagros Food Co. *Mexican* ▽ 20 | 15 | 21 | $24

Paia | 3 Baldwin Ave. (Hana Hwy.) | 808-579-8755 | milagrosfoodcompany.com

"Generous portions" of "down-home Mexican with a healthy flair" (including "super-good" huevos rancheros at breakfast) and an "amazing selection of tequilas" help make up for digs that are "nothing to write home about" at this Paia cantina; for "pure entertainment", regulars recommend watching the "hippies, surfers, wannabe rastas and tourists go by" over a cold beer or "margarita on the patio."

Nick's Fishmarket *Seafood* 23 | 23 | 23 | $63

Wailea | Fairmont Kea Lani | 4100 Wailea Alanui Dr. (Kaukahi St.) | 808-879-7224 | www.tristarrestaurants.com

"Now you are talking seafood" exclaim enthusiasts over the "imaginative preparations" of "fresh" fin fare at this maritimer at the

Fairmont Kea Lani in Wailea, which offers a "beautiful view" of the resort's "opulent" grounds from its "romantic" Med-accented interior and "magical" outdoor patio; an "extensive wine list" and "impeccable" service round out the "outstanding" experience, though cognoscenti caution "you'll leave feeling lighter" - in the "wallet", that is.

'Ono Bar & Grill *American/Hawaiian* 19 | 21 | 21 | $35

Kaanapali | Westin Maui Resort & Spa | 2365 Kaanapali Pkwy. (bet. Kekaa Dr. & Nohea Kai Dr.) | 808-667-2525 | www.westinmaui.com

"Pleasant service", a "pretty" poolside setting under thatched umbrellas and "tasty" American eats "using local ingredients" make this all-day eatery "worth a visit even when one is not staying" at the Westin Maui declare fans; naysayers, though, contend it "fills a need rather than a thirst" and find "nothing special" about it, save its "location in one of the best resorts on Kaanapali Beach."

Outback Steakhouse *Steak* 18 | 16 | 19 | $33

Kihei | 281 Piikea Ave. (Liloa Dr.) | 808-879-8400

Lahaina | Lahaina Gateway Ctr. | 325 Keawe St. (Honoapiilani Hwy.) | 808-665-1822

www.outback.com

See review in Oahu Directory.

Pacific'O *Pacific Rim/Seafood* 25 | 24 | 23 | $55

Lahaina | 505 Front St. (Shaw St.) | 808-667-4341 | www.pacificomaui.com

The "freshness is apparent" in the "locally caught fish" just "off the boat" and "organic ingredients grown Upcountry" that go into chef James McDonald's "impeccably prepared" Pacific Rim cuisine at this "fantastic beachfront restaurant" in Lahaina, where "unbeatable" sunsets, "friendly" service and "wonderful nightly jazz" add to the allure; while some find it "overpriced", many others conclude that it's "always worth a visit."

Paia Fish Market *Seafood* 26 | 14 | 16 | $22

Paia | 2 Baldwin Ave. (bet. Mahika St. & Paia Mill Rd.) | 808-579-8030 | www.paiafishmarket.com

Finatics "dream about" this "inexpensive" Paia seafooder serving "awesome fish burgers" and other "fabulous" fruits de mer "just out of the water" in a "no-frills" "cafeteria-like" setting where you "order at the counter and pick up" your meal, then join the "locals, tourists and surfers" sitting "cheek by jowl" at "communal tables"; despite "long lines", for many it's a "must-do in Maui."

Peggy Sue's *Diner* ∇ 21 | 18 | 22 | $20

Kihei | Azeka II Shopping Ctr. | 1279 S. Kihei Rd. (bet. E. Lipoa St. & Pikea Ave.) | 808-875-8944 | www.peggysues-maui.com

"Inexpensive" "juicy burgers", "thick, flavorful" shakes and "delicious chocolate malts" served by a "friendly" staff make this Kihei diner/coffee-shop "throwback to the '50s" a "family favorite"; the "shopping-center location" isn't as exciting as the trip "back in time."

Penne Pasta Cafe *Italian* 20 | 11 | 17 | $21

Lahaina | 180 Dickenson St. (Wainee St.) | 808-661-6633 | www.pennepastacafe.com

Loyalists "love" this "little local" "secret" in Lahaina that proffers some of the "tastiest Italian" on Maui; it's "not gourmet", mind you, but the pasta, pizzas and sandwiches are "great for the price", so "get a table on the patio" and enjoy the "pleasant, unhurried" service.

Pineapple Grill *Pacific Rim* 25 | 23 | 24 | $51

Kapalua | Kapalua Resort | 200 Kapalua Dr. (bet. Office Rd. & Pineapple Rd.) | 808-669-9600 | www.pineapplekapalua.com

"Get a table by the window and watch the sunset" over the fairways at this "beautiful" Kapalua Resort eatery where the "innovative" Pacific Rim menu "masterfully incorporates local ingredients" (try the "out-of-this-world pineapple upside down cake" or "extraordinary" short ribs); with "wonderful" service and "excellent" ambiance to boot, this one's "awesome" from "soup to nuts"; P.S. go for the "bargain, half-price pupus" on certain days.

Plantation House *Mediterranean* 25 | 26 | 25 | $52

Kapalua | Plantation Golf Course | 2000 Plantation Club Dr. (Honoapiilani Hwy.) | 808-669-6299 | www.theplantationhouse.com

A "spectacular" setting "overlooking the Plantation Golf Course with views to the ocean" prompts patrons to arrive at this "elegant" Kapalua Mediterranean in time for "killer sunsets"; "fabulous" locally driven fare, including some of "Maui's best fish preparations", and "impeccable" service explain the high prices, though it's less expensive "for breakfast, lunch" and an "absolutely delectable" brunch.

Round Table Pizza *Pizza* 19 | 11 | 15 | $19

Kaanapali | Fairway Shops | 2580 Kekaa Dr. (Kualapa Loop) | 808-662-0777
Kihei | 207 Piikea Ave. (Liloa Dr.) | 808-874-8485
www.roundtablepizza.com
See review in Oahu Directory.

Z Roy's *Hawaii Reg.* 26 | 22 | 24 | $55

Lahaina | Kahana Gateway Shopping Ctr. | 4405 Honoapiilani Hwy. (Hoohui Rd.) | 808-669-6999 | www.roysrestaurant.com
See review in Oahu Directory.

Ruby's *Diner* ▽ 20 | 19 | 21 | $21

Kahului | Queen Kaahumanu Ctr. | 275 W. Kaahumanu Ave. (S. Wakea Ave.) | 808-248-7829 | www.rubys.com

Tot-toting touters of this "consistent" nationwide chain of 1940s-style diners say "you've got to try this location" in Kahului's Queen Kaahumanu Center, since you're "guaranteed the kids will like" something on the "basic" American menu; a staff that "cares" delivers "enjoyable" breakfasts, "messy burgers", 20 types of "delicious", "thick shakes" and a heavy lineup of salads, sandwiches and seafood.

Ruth's Chris Steak House *Steak* 25 | 22 | 25 | $63

Lahaina | Lahaina Ctr. | 900 Front St. (bet. Baker & Papalaua Sts.) | 808-661-8815
Wailea | Shops at Wailea | 3750 Wailea Alanui Dr. (Wailea Ike Dr.) | 808-874-8880
www.ruthschris.com
See review in Oahu Directory.

Z Sansei *Japanese/Pacific Rim* 25 | 18 | 22 | $46

Kapalua | Kapalua Resort | 600 Office Rd. (Lower Honoapiilani Rd.) | 808-669-6286
Kihei | Kihei Town Ctr. | 1881 S. Kihei Rd. (Halelani Pl.) | 808-879-0004
www.sanseihawaii.com
See review in Oahu Directory.

	FOOD	DECOR	SERVICE	COST

Sarento's on the Beach *Mediterranean*

25 | 25 | 25 | $58

Kihei | 2980 S. Kihei Rd. (Kilohana Dr.) | 808-875-7555 | www.tristarrestaurants.com

It's "a little out of the way", but "when they say 'on the beach' they mean it" report regulars who "reach out and touch the sand" while soaking in "gorgeous sunset views" at this "romantic" Kihei Mediterranean, sister to Waikiki's Sarento's Top of the 'I'; the "wonderful" food, "generous portions" and "attentive" service are almost as good as the "sound of the crashing waves."

Sea House *Pacific Rim*

22 | 22 | 23 | $44

Napili | Napili Kai Beach Resort | 5900 Lower Honoapiilani Rd. (Honoapiilani Hwy.) | 808-669-1500 | www.napilikai.com

Being "on the bay" has its advantages admit admirers of this sandside Pacific Rim veteran in Maui's Napili Kai Resort, since you can "snorkel right after" downing "awesome eggs Benedict" for breakfast or "feel the cool ocean breeze" while watching "postcard-perfect", happy-hour sunsets; "live music", "wonderful service" and a few "transporting" dishes (poke nachos, for instance) make up for a "not particularly adventurous" menu.

Z Son'z at Swan Court *Seafood/Steak*

24 | 27 | 26 | $58

Kaanapali | Hyatt Regency Maui | 200 Nohea Kai Dr. (Kaanapali Pkwy.) | 808-667-4506 | www.maui.hyatt.com

With a "romantic", open-air design "overlooking black swans and a waterfall", this "beautiful" surf 'n' turfer in the Hyatt Regency Maui is "the place to propose marriage or celebrate an anniversary"; lovebirds cite the "impeccable service", "amazing" fare (which includes a "fabulous Sunday brunch") and one of "the best wine cellars on the island" as reasons it's "worth waiting for."

Z Spago *Californian/Pacific Rim*

26 | 27 | 26 | $76

(aka Wolfgang Puck's Spago Maui)

Wailea | Four Seasons Resort Maui at Wailea | 3900 Wailea Alanui Dr. (Wailea Ike Dr.) | 808-879-2999 | www.wolfgangpuck.com

The Four Seasons Wailea outpost of Wolfgang Puck's well-known chain (Maui's No. 1 for Decor) is "so much better than his other locations" say fans who cite "fantastic sunsets", "fabulous" California-Pacific Rim fare and service so "superb" the "busboys know more about wine than head waiters everywhere else"; the "refined setting", including a "lovely terrace", regularly attracts "a celebrity or two"; P.S. don't miss the "decadent" ahi tuna poke in sesame miso cones.

Stella Blues *American* 20 | 17 | 20 | $29

Kihei | Azeka Mauka Shopping Ctr. | 1279 S. Kihei Rd. (bet. E. Lipoa St. & Piikea Ave.) | 808-874-3779 | www.stellablues.com

"Grateful Dead fans" have "found a home" at this Kihei comfort-food "favorite" with a "'60s" vibe that extends to the "schizo menu" of "upscale diner food" offering "anything from steak and potatoes to tofu and sprouts" (as well as vegan options); other pluses include a "solid breakfast", live entertainment on weekends and "fast service."

Tokyo Tei *Japanese* ▽ 20 | 11 | 18 | $26

Wailuku | 1063 Lower Main St. (bet. Koni & Pua Pls.) | 808-242-9630

"Delicately prepared tempura", katsu that's "crisp on the outside, moist inside" and a miso butterfish that's "just right" are draws at this "mom-and-pop" Japanese in Wailuku; expect a "sweet staff" and a "strictly local" crowd, but "don't come for the atmosphere."

Tommy Bahama's *Asian/Caribbean* 21 | 23 | 21 | $45

Wailea | Shops at Wailea | 3750 Wailea Alanui Dr. (Wailea Ike Dr.) | 808-875-9983 | www.tommybahama.com

Serving "extremely large portions" of Caribbean-Asian fusion fare at its branches on Maui and the Big Island, this mini-chain affiliated with the tropical clothing store is a "predictable" spot for "otherworldly" "drinks that get you in the island spirit", "terrific early-birds", "sunset pupus" and a "fun crowd"; but those who cite "forced", "kitschy" interiors, "slow" service and "noisy" settings say "Tommy should stick to clothes."

Umalu ◐ *Hawaii Reg.* ▽ 22 | 23 | 21 | $34

Kaanapali | Hyatt Regency Maui | 200 Nohea Kai Dr. (Kaanapali Pkwy.) | 808-667-4902 | www.maui.hyatt.com

You can "get up and walk to the ocean" from your seat at this indoor/outdoor eatery in the Hyatt Regency resort in Kaanapali, where chef

Kevin Boyle cooks up a "pleasantly surprising" Hawaii Regional menu; fans single out the "terrific" burgers, fries and wraps, "spicy ahi nachos" and "quick, friendly" service, recommending it for "sunset pupus" with "live music"; sure, it's "expensive", but "what do you expect poolside on Maui?"

Waterfront Restaurant *Seafood* 25 | 22 | 23 | $56

Maalaea | 50 Hauoli St. (Maalaea Rd.) | 808-244-9028 | www.waterfrontrestaurant.net

It's a "bit of a surprise" to find "tuxedo-clad waiters" in Hawaii, but here they are, "treating you like family", at this long-standing fish house in Maalaea, where the seafood "can't get any fresher" and the "excellent Caesar salad" is "prepared tableside"; the decor and approach may be "too old-school" for trendsetters, but it's hard to argue with those "peaceful sunset views" from a "lovely lanai overlooking the harbor."

FOOD | DECOR | SERVICE | COST

Big Island

TOP FOOD

26 Pahu i'a | *Hawaii Reg./Seafood*
Merriman's | *Hawaii Reg.*
Hilo Bay Café | *Pacific Rim*
La Bourgogne | *French*
Roy's | *Hawaii Reg.*

TOP DECOR

28 Pahu i'a
27 CanoeHouse
Brown's Beach Hse.
Manta/Pavilion Wine
25 Beach Tree B&G

TOP SERVICE

26 Pahu i'a
25 Merriman's
La Bourgogne
Beach Tree B&G
Ruth's Chris

BEST BUYS

1. Cafe 100
2. Maui Tacos
3. Manago Hotel
4. Big Island Grill
5. Teshima's

Bamboo M *Pacific Rim* 23 22 24 $34

Hawi | Hwy. 270 (Hwy. 250) | 808-889-5555 | www.bamboorestaurant.info

The "cheerful" staff provides a "warm example of the aloha spirit" at this "hidden gem" in Hawi, a "reincarnated sugar town" in a "remote corner" of the Big Island, where "locals and tourists" alike head for "terrific" Pacific Rim fare and some of the "best mai tais in the islands"; the decor is pure "Hawaiian kitsch" in the "historic building", and on evenings when "Grammy-winner John Keawe" plays slack key guitar and "his wife, Hope, gives hula lessons", fans declare it "old Hawaii at its best."

Beach Tree Bar & Grill *Californian/Italian* 24 25 25 $49

Kaupulehu-Kona | Four Seasons Resort Hualalai | 72-100 Kaupulehu Dr. (Kumukehu St.) | 808-325-8000 | www.fourseasons.com

For "beachside dining at its best", fans tout the "opulent" Four Seasons Hualalai's outdoor Cal-Italian in an "unbeatable setting" "just steps from the ocean", with a "newly remodeled" look that's at once "casual and sophisticated"; sure, it's "pricey", but with an "attentive" staff that "remembers your name", "delightfully prepared" cuisine, "excellent cocktails" and "incredible views", almost all regard it as a "worthy splurge."

BIG ISLAND

FOOD | DECOR | SERVICE | COST

Big Island Grill *American*

FOOD	DECOR	SERVICE	COST
21	16	20	$20

Kailua-Kona | 75-5702 Kuakini Hwy. (bet. Hanama Pl. & Henry St.) | 808-326-1153

This "casual" Kailua-Kona coffee shop is "where the locals eat when they want really big portions" of "reasonably priced" "Hawaiian-style" American "diner food"; service is "fast" but "not pushy", and while some sniff that the "decor has seen better days", it's still a "nice choice" and a "good value" in the minds of many.

Brown's Beach House *Seafood*

FOOD	DECOR	SERVICE	COST
24	27	24	$63

Kohala Coast | Fairmont Orchid | 1 N. Kaniku Dr. (S. Kaniku Dr.) | Kamuela | 808-885-2000 | www.fairmont.com/orchid

An "exquisite" oceanfront setting with a "magnificent tiki torch-lit view" of the "beautiful lagoon and beach", "terrific live music" and "hula dancers" - "this is what you go to Hawaii for" sigh fans of this seafood specialist in the Kohala Coast's Fairmont Orchid; the "superb", "island-fresh" fin fare, "professional" service and "romantic" setting are all suitable for "that special occasion", but like any "true tropical experience", it's "expensive" (though the "early-bird menu is a very good deal").

Bubba Gump Shrimp Co. *American/Seafood*

FOOD	DECOR	SERVICE	COST
16	18	18	$28

Kailua-Kona | 75-5776 Alii Dr. (Hualalai Rd.) | 808-331-8442 | www.bubbagump.com

See review in Oahu Directory.

Buzz's Sand Trap *Steak*

FOOD	DECOR	SERVICE	COST
20	20	20	$35

Waikoloa | 69-1022 Keana Pl. (Waikoloa Beach Dr.) | 808-886-8797 | www.buzzssandtrap.com

See review in Oahu Directory.

Cafe 100 *American/Hawaiian*

FOOD	DECOR	SERVICE	COST
20	10	19	$9

Hilo | 969 Kilauea Ave. (Maile St.) | 808-935-8683

This "really local" Hilo spot (the purported "home of the loco moco") "puts the fast in fast food", dishing out "tasty plate lunches" of Hawaiian and American fare; "don't expect much in the way of decor" unless you "go out back and sit on the grass along the lagoon", but given the "cheap", "satisfying" eats, few are complaining.

FOOD	DECOR	SERVICE	COST

Café Pesto *Eclectic* 23 | 18 | 21 | $32

Hilo | Historic S. Hata Bldg. | 308 Kamehameha Ave. (bet. Haili & Mamo Sts.) | 808-969-6640
Kawaihae Harbor | Kawaihae Harbor Ctr. | 61-3665 Hwy. 270 (Kohala Mountain Rd.) | Kamuela | 808-882-1071
www.cafepesto.com

A "reasonable option" for local families and tourists "tired of hotel offerings" and their "exhausting prices", this Eclectic duo on the Big Island offers a "taste of Italy mixed with local" influences, including "outstanding" pizzas, "wonderful, fresh" seafood and "innovative" salads, delivered by "solicitous" servers in "casual, comfortable" settings; the Hilo location boasts an airy, "high-ceilinged" space, and while some say the "view is not the best" at the Kawaihae branch, at least it's fairly "close to the Waikoloa beaches."

Z CanoeHouse S M *Eclectic* 24 | 27 | 24 | $64

Kohala Coast | Mauna Lani Resort | 68-1400 Mauna Lani Dr. (Mauna Lani Ter.) | Kamuela | 808-881-7911 | www.maunalani.com

Fans are in "absolute heaven" at the Mauna Lani Resort's Eclectic restaurant, located in an "exquisite setting" "along the prettiest coastline in Kohala", where you "can't lose" whether seated inside the "elegant, upscale" dining room or outside with the "waves at your feet"; "beautifully presented" cuisine and an "excellent" wine list are served by a "friendly, professional" staff, and while some "just wish it weren't so expensive", many conclude it's "worth the splurge."

Coast Grille *Pacific Rim* 21 | 22 | 21 | $56

Kohala Coast | Hapuna Beach Prince Hotel | 62-100 Kaunaoa Dr. (Old Puako Rd.) | Kamuela | 808-880-3023 | www.princeresortshawaii.com

Situated in "peaceful surroundings" with "lovely" views, this Pacific Rim spot at the Kohala Coast's Hapuna Beach Prince Hotel is a "nice place to end the day" with a "beautiful sunset" and a mai tai; its "elegantly prepared dishes" are delivered by a generally "attentive" staff, though some consider the fare "just ok for the price" and believe the "service could be kicked up a notch."

Daniel Thiebaut *Asian/Hawaii Reg.* 24 | 21 | 21 | $51

Waimea | 65-1259 Kawaihae Rd. (Lindsey Rd.) | 808-887-2200 | www.danielthiebaut.com

The "location is as quaint as the food is spectacular" at Daniel Thiebaut's Hawaii Regional-Pan-Asian in Waimea, housed in a "cleverly" restored general store, where "inventive dishes using fresh local ingredients", including "excellent" seafood offerings, and an "overflowing" brunch spread are a "delight to the senses", while the staff is "friendly"; a few are "disappointed" by "inconsistent" cooking and service, but most consider it "worth the trip Upcountry."

Don the Beachcomber *Pacific Rim* 17 | 23 | 18 | $37

Kailua-Kona | Royal Kona Resort | 75-5852 Alii Dr. (bet. Hualalai & Lunapule Rds.) | 808-329-3111 | www.royalkona.com

A "beautiful location right on the water" with "fabulous" sunset views, tiki decor that evokes the "old flavor of Hawaii" and a "wonderful drink menu" are the big draws at this "tourist mecca" in the Royal Kona Resort, the purported "birthplace of the mai tai"; most regard the Pacific Rim fare as "decent hotel food", though some find it "forgettable except for the high, high prices" and quip that you'll "age dramatically while waiting" to be served.

Hale Samoa *French/Pacific Rim* ∇ 20 | 22 | 22 | $78

Kailua-Kona | Kona Village Resort | Queen Kaahumanu Hwy. (Melelina St.) | 808-325-5555 | www.konavillage.com

"You can't get any closer to the ocean" than this French-Pacific Rim eatery in Kailua-Kona's Kona Village Resort - aficionados prefer to "sit outside" where "you feel like you're right on the beach" and take in "sunset views to die for"; while fans praise the fare as "high quality", cynics dismiss it as "nothing special for the price", though most agree the "spectacular" setting makes it a "good hot-date spot."

Hilo Bay Café *Pacific Rim* 26 | 19 | 24 | $32

Hilo | Waiakea Shopping Ctr. | 315 Makaala St. (bet. Kanoelehuna Ave. & Pohaku St.) | 808-935-4939 | www.hilobaycafe.com

The "strip-mall location" of this Hilo Pacific Rim spot may make you "skeptical at first", but once inside, it's "first-class dining" all the way thanks to "outstanding", "creative" cuisine ("on par with upscale resort fare") served by an "accommodating" staff in a "modern, simple" space; "good value" is another reason why its "mostly local" following considers it a "beacon" of "sophisticated dining."

Huggos *Pacific Rim/Seafood* 21 | 22 | 20 | $42

Kailua-Kona | 75-5828 Kahakai Rd. (Alii Dr.) | 808-329-1493 | www.huggos.com

Stalwarts have "never been disappointed" by this "longtime favorite" in Kailua-Kona where the "fantastic" setting with a "million-dollar view" of the ocean makes many overlook the "tiki" decor; fans praise the "excellent variety" of Pacific Rim "small and large plates", "fresh fish" and "helpful" service (the "nightly entertainment is appreciated" too), but dissenters find the menu "not inspired" and rail that some staffers have "gotten too big for their britches."

Imari *Japanese* ▽ 22 | 23 | 21 | $64

Kohala Coast | Hilton Waikoloa Vill. | 425 Waikoloa Beach Dr. (Queen Kaahumanu Hwy.) | Kamuela | 808-886-1234 | www.hiltonwaikoloavillage.com

Japanophiles "love the decor" of this "upscale" Japanese in the Kohala Coast's Hilton Waikoloa Village, where kimono, shoji and Imari porcelain adorn the updated traditional space, which overlooks a koi pond; the "excellent menu" includes a range of offerings from sushi to teppanyaki, but some critics feel it "caters to the American palate" and is "overpriced" to boot.

Jackie Rey's Ohana Grill *Eclectic* 24 | 17 | 24 | $34

Kailua-Kona | Pottery Terr. | 75-5995 Kuakini Hwy. (Walua Rd.) | 808-327-0209 | www.jackiereys.com

"Tucked away in an office plaza", this Kailua-Kona Eclectic is "where the locals eat" (though "tourists are welcome too") for an "adventuresome menu" of "well-prepared dishes" (including "excellent seafood") for roughly "half as much dinero as you'd pay on the seashore"; the "friendly" servers who "treat you like family" are clearly "having fun - and it's infectious", while the cheery decor is "authentic Kona."

	FOOD	DECOR	SERVICE	COST
Kamuela Provision Company *Pacific Rim*	21	24	21	$50

Kohala Coast | Hilton Waikoloa Vill. | 425 Waikoloa Beach Dr. (Queen Kaahumanu Hwy.) | Kamuela | 808-886-1234 | www.hiltonwaikoloavillage.com

"Sit outdoors to get the full effect" of the "waves crashing" and the "most beautiful sunset" at this Pacific Rim surf 'n' turf specialist in the Kohala Coast's Hilton Waikoloa Village; if a few find the menu "uninventive" and "expensive for what it is", carnivores crow the kitchen "really knows how to prepare a slab of meat" and it's delivered with generally "very good" service.

	FOOD	DECOR	SERVICE	COST
Keei Café *Eclectic*	24	23	20	$41

Kealakekua | 79-7511 Mamalahoa Hwy. (Hokukano Rd.) | 808-322-9992

While it offers "no particular view", this Kealakekua Eclectic is "well worth visiting" for its "wide variety" of "imaginative", "reasonably priced" dishes with "wonderful Asian-Pacific flavors", served by a "friendly, helpful" staff; the "out-of-the-way" location is "easy to drive past", so "locals and tourists" alike are advised to "slow down" for some of the "best bargain high-end food on the Big Island."

	FOOD	DECOR	SERVICE	COST
Kenichi Pacific *Asian/Japanese*	24	19	22	$44

Keauhou | Keauhou Shopping Ctr. | 78-6831 Alii Dr. (Kamehameha III Rd.) | Kailua-Kona | 808-322-6400 | www.kenichihawaii.com

The "half-price sushi is hard to beat" at this Keauhou Japanese, which also serves "innovative" Asian fusion fare "prepared and served with style"; maybe the "shopping-mall" location is "not the best" and it's sometimes "noisy", but fans say the "terrific" staff and "reasonable prices" compensate.

	FOOD	DECOR	SERVICE	COST
Kiawe Kitchen *Mediterranean/Pacific Rim*	∇ 23	16	17	$31

Volcano | 19-4005 Haunani Rd. (Old Volcano Rd.) | 808-967-7711

This "cute little" spot "caters to lava lookers" with "delicious" wood-fired pizzas, "great lamb entrees" and other Med-Pacific Rim offerings that are "perfect for the Volcano climate"; some find it a bit "overpriced" and gripe about "interminable wait times", but others insist the fare and "fun cocktails" are "worth it."

	FOOD	DECOR	SERVICE	COST

Kilauea Lodge *Eclectic*

21	22	21	$44

Volcano | Kilauea Lodge | 19-3948 Old Volcano Rd. (bet. Kalanikoa St. & Post Office Ln.) | 808-967-7366 | www.kilauealodge.com

A "beautiful fireplace enhances the warm atmosphere" of this "woodsy", "hunting lodge-style" Eclectic eatery located in a "former YMCA camp" in Volcano's Kilauea Village, where the kitchen turns out a "German-Hawaiian fusion that works"; some feel the service "could be quicker" and find the tabs "pricey", but for many, the "rarified setting makes it worth the extra few dollars (and the drive)."

Kona Brewing Co. *American*

20	19	19	$26

Kailua-Kona | 75-5629 Kuakini Hwy. (Palani Rd.) | 808-329-2739 | www.konabrewingco.com

"World-class beers", "wonderful, hand-tossed" pizzas and "commendable" pub grub draw "hungry Hawaiians and tourists" to this microbrew twosome on the Big Island and Oahu; though critics complain of "un-aloha-like greetings" and "slacker" service, most applaud the "fun pub atmosphere" and "occasional live music" at the Kailua-Kona branch, and Hawaii Kai's "great location by the water."

Kona Inn Restaurant *Seafood*

20	24	21	$35

Kailua-Kona | Kona Inn Shopping Vill. | 75-5744 Alii Dr. (Hualalai Rd.) | 808-329-4455 | www.konainnrestaurant.com

Fans insist this "charming" seafooder "should be on every visitor's list" thanks mainly to its "wonderful" oceanfront location at the Kona Inn Shopping Village in Kailua-Kona, offering "unbelievable views of the surf"; "friendly" service, "fresh" fin fare "done simply and perfectly" and some of the "best mai tais in the Hawaiian islands" seal the deal.

La Bourgogne Ⓢ Ⓜ *French*

26	20	25	$57

Kailua-Kona | 77-6400 Nalani St. (Kuakini Hwy.) | 808-329-6711

"Step into another world - and don't order a mai tai" - at this "family-run" Kailua-Kona Gallic where the "charming, gracious" owners "make you feel at home", offering "outstanding" "country French" cuisine, "served beautifully and elegantly" and backed by a "substantial wine list" with "very low markups"; the "small, intimate" setting has a "romantic", "old-world feel", and even though there's "no outdoor seating", many regard it as a "must-go-to place."

Manago Hotel M *American/Hawaiian* 21 | 14 | 22 | $19

Captain Cook | Manago Hotel | 82-6155 Mamalahoa Hwy. (Kinue Rd.) | 808-323-2642 | www.managohotel.com

If you want to "experience local-style *kau kau* (eats) and aloha" or simply crave "the best pork chops anywhere", fans recommend this hotel "mess hall" in Captain Cook that'll "take you back to the plantation era" with its "creaky wooden floors", "wash basin" and "old-school vibe"; "straight-up" American-Hawaiian victuals (including "family-style sides"), "very friendly" service and "bargain prices" make it a "must-do in Kona" for many.

Manta & Pavilion Wine Bar *Hawaii Reg.* 25 | 27 | 25 | $66

Kohala Coast | Mauna Kea Beach Hotel | 62-100 Mauna Kea Beach Dr. (Hwy. 19) | Kamuela | 808-882-7222 | www.princeresortshawaii.com

The Kohala Coast's Mauna Kea Beach Hotel "now has a restaurant equal to the perfection" of its "beautiful location" "overlooking the gorgeous beach and bay", offering "fantastic", "creative" Hawaii Regional cuisine, including "amazing brunches", and "dedicated", "professional" service; the atmosphere is "surprisingly child-friendly for such a romantic place" ("kids love the nightly dance of the manta rays in the ocean below"), and the "wine tasting bar is a real plus."

Maui Tacos *Mexican* 19 | 8 | 14 | $13

Hilo | Prince Kuhio Plaza | 111 E. Puainako St. (off Hawaii Belt Rd.) | 808-959-0359 | www.mauitacos.com

See review in Maui Directory.

Z **Merriman's** *Hawaii Reg.* 26 | 24 | 25 | $60

Waimea | Opelo Plaza | 65-1227 Opelo Rd. (bet. Kawaihae Rd. & Pomaikai Pl.) | 808-885-6822 | www.merrimanshawaii.com

"About the best the Big Island has to offer", and voted its Most Popular restaurant, Peter Merriman's "magical" Waimea Hawaii Regional is "well worth the trip to cowboy country" for "incredible farm-to-table cuisine" made with "local, sustainable" ingredients and complemented by an "outstanding" wine list full of "hidden treasures", all served by a "thoughtful", "professional" staff in a "homey" ambiance; the Maui sibling boasts a "beautiful setting near Kapalua Beach", while the seafood-centric Koloa branch is "setting a new standard" on Kauai.

Merriman's Market Café *Mediterranean* 21 | 17 | 19 | $34

Waikoloa | Kings' Shops | 69-250 Waikoloa Beach Dr. (off Hwy. 19) | 808-886-1700

A "rare find" in a "high-rent district", Peter Merriman's "unpretentious gem" in Waikoloa's Kings' Shops is the favorite choice of many for a "quick, not-too-expensive casual meal" of Med fare made with "local farm-fresh ingredients", served by an "on-the-ball" staff in a "lovely courtyard" setting that feels like a "little country bistro"; devotees of his Waimea flagship, however, sniff that it's "fine for a shopping center, but nowhere near the great experience of the original."

Monettes *American/French* 24 | 25 | 21 | $88

Kohala Coast | Mauna Kea Beach Hotel | 62-100 Mauna Kea Beach Dr. (Hwy. 19) | Kamuela | 808-443-2850 | www.monetteshawaii.com

A "beautiful setting" with "wonderful sunsets" is the backdrop for this "elegant" Franco-American in the Mauna Kea Beach Hotel overlooking Kauna'oa Bay on the Kohala Coast, where "creative", "classic and nouvelle" cooking and a "great wine list" "impress" fans; still, some feel that it "has yet to define itself", resulting in "hit-or-miss" food and "service that needs work", though "when it's on, it is amazing."

NEW **Monstera** *Japanese/Hawaii Reg.* - | - | - | E

Kohala Coast | The Shops at Mauna Lani | 68-1330 Mauna Lani Dr. (Kaniku Dr.) | Kamuela | 808-887-2711 | www.monsterasushi.com

Chef Norio Yamamoto (ex Norio's Japanese at the Fairmont Orchid) opened this Japanese-Hawaii Regional just down the street from his former gig in The Shops at Mauna Lani mall, where an eclectic menu that includes sushi, grilled fare, noodles and small plates is served in a spacious, low-key room with stained concrete flooring and whitewashed walls adorned with colorful artwork; it also boasts a generous selection of sake, shochu and Hawaiian cocktails.

	FOOD	DECOR	SERVICE	COST

Norio's Japanese Restaurant & Sushi Bar *Japanese* — 24 | 20 | 22 | $60

Kohala Coast | Fairmont Orchid | 1 N. Kaniku Dr. (Hoohana St.) | Kamuela | 808-887-7320 | www.fairmont.com/orchid

A "nice surprise inside the Fairmont Orchid" on the Kohala Coast, this "quiet" Japanese dishes out "wonderfully fresh" sushi and other "filling" dishes, although some say it's a "bit on the expensive side"; many also find the space "outdated" and "not much to look at", and longtime loyalists lament the departure of eponymous chef Norio Yamamoto, which may also account for a dip in the Food score.

Outback Steakhouse *Steak* — 18 | 16 | 19 | $33

Kailua-Kona | Coconut Grove Mktpl. | 75-5809 Alii Dr. (Hualalai Rd.) | 808-326-2555 | www.outback.com

See review in Oahu Directory.

Z Pahu i'a *Hawaii Reg./Seafood* — 26 | 28 | 26 | $80

Kaupulehu-Kona | Four Seasons Resort Hualalai | 72-100 Kaupulehu Dr. (Kumukehu St.) | 808-325-8000 | www.fourseasons.com

"Paradise in paradise" is how devotees describe this Hawaii Regional seafooder in North Kona's Four Seasons Hualalai, voted the Big Island's No. 1 for Food, Decor and Service, where the "exquisite" oceanfront location and "spectacular open-air dining room" set the stage for an "engaging, knowledgeable" staff serving "expertly prepared" fin fare, including "many locally sourced choices"; there's also a "deep" (if some say "overpriced") wine list and a "memorable" breakfast buffet - in sum, "everything is first-class", including the "budget-buster" tabs.

Paniolo Country Inn *Eclectic* — ▽ 20 | 15 | 19 | $20

Kamuela | 65-1214 Lindsey Rd. (Mamalahoa Hwy.) | 808-885-4377

It's "practically the only place to get breakfast in Waimea on a Sunday morning", so this "old-school", Hawaiian-style Eclectic diner in Kamuela attracts plenty of locals; expect "huge paniolo" portions, "reasonable prices" and a "comfortable" setting that some say "could use an uplift."

	FOOD	DECOR	SERVICE	COST

Quinn's Almost by the Sea *Seafood* 21 | 13 | 19 | $23

Kailua-Kona | 75-5655 Palani Rd. (Kuakini Hwy.) | 808-329-3822

Locals claim to get "the best fish 'n' chips on the island" at this "watering hole" in Kona with an "extensive" American menu of "sandwiches, steaks and seafood"; it's "hard to find parking" and, as the name implies, you'll have to "walk down the street for a harbor view", but the "lanai in back" and friendly, "hi ya hon'" service works for a "casual" bite.

Romano's Macaroni Grill *Italian* 17 | 17 | 18 | $29

Waikoloa | Queens' Mktpl. | 69-201 Waikoloa Beach Dr. (Queen Kaahumanu Hwy.) | 808-443-5515 | www.macaronigrill.com

See review in Oahu Directory.

Z Roy's *Hawaii Reg.* 26 | 22 | 24 | $55

Waikoloa | Kings' Shops | 250 Waikoloa Beach Dr. (off Hwy. 19) | 808-886-4321 | www.roysrestaurant.com

See review in Oahu Directory.

Ruth's Chris Steak House *Steak* 25 | 22 | 25 | $63

Kohala Coast | Shops at Mauna Lani | 68-1330 Mauna Lani Dr. (Kaniku Dr.) | Kamuela | 808-887-0800 | www.ruthschris.com

See review in Oahu Directory.

Z Sansei *Japanese/Pacific Rim* 25 | 18 | 22 | $46

Kohala Coast | Waikoloa Beach Resort | 69-201 Waikoloa Beach Dr. (Queen Kaahumanu Hwy.) | Kamuela | 808-886-6286 | www.sanseihawaii.com

See review in Oahu Directory.

Teshima's ≠ *Japanese* 20 | 12 | 21 | $22

Kealakekua | 79-7251 Mamalahoa Hwy. (bet. Kuakini Hwy. & St. Paul's Rd.) | 808-322-9140

"Still hanging on" after all these years, this "cash-only local" "gem" in Kealakekua dishes up "awesome" "Hawaii-style Japanese" ("killer saimin", "delicious shrimp tempura") along with a "sincere 'how are you'" to the "old-timers, farmers and fishermen" who frequent the "joint"; "almost everyone knows the Teshima family", and have learned to love the "simple" space sporting the "same self-adhesive tiles for the last 40 years."

Tommy Bahama's *Asian/Caribbean* 21 23 21 $45

Kohala Coast | Shops at Mauna Lani | 68-1330 Mauna Lani Dr. (Kaniku Dr.) | Kamuela | 808-881-8686 | www.tommybahama.com

See review in Maui Directory.

	FOOD	DECOR	SERVICE	COST

Kauai

TOP FOOD

26 Kauai Grill | *Eclectic*
Merriman's | *Hawaii Reg.*
Roy's | *Hawaii Reg.*
Red Salt | *Hawaiian*
25 Bar Acuda | *Mediterranean*

TOP DECOR

28 Kauai Grill
27 Tidepools
26 Beach House
25 Dondero's
Plantation Gardens

TOP SERVICE

25 Kauai Grill
Dondero's
Merriman's
24 Tidepools
Roy's

BEST BUYS

1. Duane's Ono-Char
2. Bubba Burgers
3. Koloa Fish Market
4. Shrimp Station
5. Kalaheo Café

Bar Acuda *Mediterranean* — 25 | 22 | 22 | $47

Hanalei | Hanalei Town Ctr. | 5-5161 Kuhio Hwy. (Aku Rd.) | 808-826-7081 | www.restaurantbaracuda.com

A "sparkling alternative to barefoot beach fare" and "more formal" hotel dining, this Hanalei Mediterranean represents a "nice blending of the tapas concept with aloha flair", offering a "sophisticated menu" of "wonderful" small plates, "fabulous mai tais" and a "reasonable selection of wine" in an "elegant, small" space with a "big-city" feel; the servers "take pride in their establishment", though critics claim they can be "too cool for thou" and grouse that you "pay too much for too little here."

Z Beach House *Pacific Rim* — 24 | 26 | 24 | $56

Poipu | 5022 Lawai Rd. (Hoona Rd.) | Koloa | 808-742-1424 | www.the-beach-house.com

"Spectacular" sunsets and "the Pacific Ocean, up close and personal", create the "inspiring", "romantic" backdrop at this Poipu Beach "classic", voted Kauai's Most Popular for its "beautiful" surroundings, "imaginative" Pacific Rim cuisine, "outstanding drinks" and "impeccable" service; though some find it "overpriced" and lament the "crazy" crowds that "rush out to get their pictures taken on the rocks", most regard it as an "incredible dining experience."

	FOOD	DECOR	SERVICE	COST
Brennecke's *American/Seafood*	19	17	19	$32

Poipu | 2100 Hoone Rd. (Poipu Rd.) | Koloa | 808-742-7588 | www.brenneckes.com

The "epitome of island casual dining", this "reasonably priced" American maritimer across the street from Poipu Beach offers one of the "best cheap sunsets" from its open-air dining room, where a "friendly" staff delivers "fresh seafood" and "solid" comfort fare; some say "potent" drinks and the "views" are what make it so "popular."

	FOOD	DECOR	SERVICE	COST
Bubba Burgers *Burgers*	19	13	18	$14

Hanalei | 5-5161 Kuhio Hwy. (Aku Rd.) | 808-826-7839
Kapaa | 4-1421 Kuhio Hwy. (Lehua St.) | 808-823-0069
NEW **Koloa** | Kukui'ula Village Mall | 2829 Ala Kalanikauamaka St. (Poipu Rd.) | 808-742-6900
www.bubbaburger.com

The "broke da mouth" eats at this trio of "casual", "old-fashioned sit-down burger-and-fries joints" on Kauai are the "perfect antidote" to "health-conscious" dining, served by an "awesome" staff that "disrespects you" in a "fun way"; while "long, slow lines" don't dissuade fans, many opt to "eat on the deck" or "take it to the beach" rather than dine in digs reminiscent of a "middle school cafeteria."

	FOOD	DECOR	SERVICE	COST
Bull Shed *Steak*	22	14	20	$36

Kapaa | 4-796 Kuhio Hwy. (Kamoa Rd.) | 808-822-3791 | www.bullshedrestaurant.com

The "BS" name notwithstanding, locals "looking for a steak dinner without breaking the bank" laud this "old family favorite" in Kapaa serving up "lots of beef" and "fresh" seafood in a "tropical casual" setting; the room's "big windows" provide a "beautiful view" of the ocean, but otherwise critics liken the space to a "retirement community rec room" and wish the staff could "be a little more personable."

	FOOD	DECOR	SERVICE	COST
Café Portofino *Italian*	22	23	22	$47

Kalapaki Beach | Kauai Marriott Resort & Beach Club | 3481 Hoolaulea Way (Westin Rd.) | Lihue | 808-245-2121 | www.cafeportofino.com

A "beautiful view" of Kalapaki Bay from "the romantic oceanfront patio" and the strains of a "harp in the background" set the tone at this Northern Italian in the Kauai Marriott, where a "happy" staff serves "tasty", "authentic" dishes backed by a "reasonable wine list"; a few critics carp over "small, overpriced portions" and "inexperienced" service, but most believe it's "worth the money."

Casablanca at Kiahuna *African/Mediterranean* 18 | 14 | 19 | $39

Poipu | Kiahuna Swim & Tennis Club | 2290 Poipu Rd. (Kiahuna Dr.) | Koloa | 808-742-2929 | www.casablancakauai.com

Newcomers are shocked, shocked to discover this "reasonably priced" "hidden gem" in an "unusual but attractive" open-air setting (with, alas, a "not-so-great view") in Poipu, where the Mediterranean-North African cuisine is a "nice departure from mainstream fare" and the servers are "eager and happy"; a few critics, though, find the experience "uneven", reporting "uninspired" cooking and "lackluster service."

Casa di Amici *Eclectic/Italian* 23 | 19 | 22 | $47

Poipu | 2301 Nalo Rd. (Hoone Rd.) | Koloa | 808-742-1555 | www.casadiamici.com

"Tucked away in a residential neighborhood" of Poipu, this "cozy beach house" is "worth finding" for its "superior" Italian-Eclectic cuisine "with an island flair" prepared by a "highly trained chef" and served by a "friendly, helpful" staff; while the interior may be "small", there's "lovely" outdoor seating offering "romantic views of the sunset."

Z Dondero's S M *Italian* 25 | 25 | 25 | $60

Poipu | Grand Hyatt | 1571 Poipu Rd. (Alnako St.) | Koloa | 808-742-1234 | www.kauai.hyatt.com

It's "fine dining all the way" at this Northern Italian situated in Poipu's Grand Hyatt Kauai, where the cuisine is "out of this world", the service is "impeccable" and the "gorgeous" interior has a "Tuscan feel", though a few find the decor "over the top" and advise sitting outside to escape the "sensory overload" (where it's "more romantic", anyway); it's "expensive", to be sure, but for the "heavenly" experience, many find the prices "shockingly reasonable."

Restaurant	Food	Decor	Service	Cost
Duane's Ono-Char Burger *Burgers*	24	8	16	$12

Anahola | 4-4350 Kuhio Hwy. (Aliomanu Rd.) | 808-822-9181

Fans of this Anahola American "roadside stand" gladly sit at outdoor "concrete tables" with "chickens running underfoot" for "one of the best hamburgers on the islands", plus "excellent fries" and "killer milkshakes"; it's "not fast food" by any means, so "be prepared to stand in line", and those who cry foul at the feathered company "can take it to the beach instead."

Restaurant	Food	Decor	Service	Cost
Duke's Canoe Club *American*	20	23	20	$34

Kalapaki Beach | Kauai Marriott Resort & Beach Club | 3610 Rice St. (Hoolaulea Way) | Lihue | 808-246-9599 | www.dukeskauai.com

See review in Oahu Directory.

Restaurant	Food	Decor	Service	Cost
Genki Sushi *Japanese*	16	13	16	$22

Lihue | Kukui Grove Shopping Ctr. | 3-2600 Kaumualii Hwy. (Nawiliwili Rd.) | 808-632-2450 | www.genkisushiusa.com

See review in Oahu Directory.

Restaurant	Food	Decor	Service	Cost
Hanalei Dolphin *Seafood*	23	19	20	$43

Hanalei | Hanalei Dolphin Ctr. | 5-5016 Kuhio Hwy. (Hanalei Bridge) | 808-826-6113 | www.hanaleidolphin.com

This Hanalei seafooder's "popularity is well deserved" according to "locals" who flock here for "flavorful" preparations of what some say is the "freshest fish on Kauai", as well as "unique rolls and nigiri" prepared by "sushi chefs who are fun to chat with"; the rest of the staff is "friendly and prompt", and while the "island-casual decor" strikes some as "nothing special", the "outdoor tables alongside the river provide a lovely setting" for lunch.

Restaurant	Food	Decor	Service	Cost
Hanalei Gourmet *American/Eclectic*	21	14	18	$29

Hanalei | Hanalei Town Ctr. | 5-5161 Kuhio Hwy. (Aku Rd.) | 808-826-2524 | www.hanaleigourmet.com

"One of the better ones" on the North Shore of Kauai, this "adorable one-room restaurant" in Hanalei is a "solid" choice for lunch and dinner and a "great place to star-watch", where you might spot some "celebrity dressed as grungily as possible" tucking into "fantastic" burgers, sandwiches and other American-Eclectic offerings from a "big menu"; "friendly" service and "local" live music are added pluses, and while some find it "too noisy inside", you can always "sit on the porch."

Hanamaulu Cafe *Japanese/Tearoom* ∇ 22 | 19 | 20 | $30

Lihue | 3-4291 Kuhio Hwy. (Hanamaulu Rd.) | 808-245-2511

Trailblazers say it's "fun to try to find" this "country" Japanese tearoom that's "totally off the beaten path" in Lihue, serving "delightful" fare including "must-have" ginger chicken or shrimp; in addition to the main dining area, there's a sushi bar and tatami rooms that "overlook beautiful gardens."

Hanapepe Café [S] *Bakery/Vegetarian* 22 | 17 | 19 | $26

Hanapepe | 3830 Hanapepe Rd. (Kona Rd.) | 808-335-5011

"Breakfast is always a winner" at this "gem" of a cafe in the "artist community" of Hanapepe, serving "wonderful vegetarian and vegan options", including "terrific homemade soups" and "daily delights" from its "excellent bakery", in a plantation-style setting with a "relaxed island vibe" and nightly live music; a few find it "a little pricey for such an out-of-the-way place" and warn of "strange hours", so if you're traveling, "be sure to call ahead"; it serves dinner on Friday nights.

Kalaheo Café & Coffee Co. *Coffeehouse* 23 | 19 | 22 | $22

Kalaheo | 2-2560 Kaumualii Hwy. (Silva Tract Rd.) | 808-332-5858 | www.kalaheo.com

Situated "along a busy, noisy highway" in an otherwise "chill location", this Kalaheo cafe dishes out "melt-in-your-mouth delicious" baked goods, "wonderful" coffee and "terrific" breakfasts and lunches; the staff conveys the "aloha spirit" to the crowd of "locals and tourists", but otherwise, you "seat yourself, stand in line to order and get your own coffee refills" in the "leisurely" setting; it also serves dinner Wednesdays-Saturdays.

[Z] [NEW] Kauai Grill [S] [M] *Eclectic* 26 | 28 | 25 | $72

Princeville | St. Regis Princeville Hotel | 5520 Ka Haku Rd. (Liholiho Rd.) | 808-826-9644 | www.stregisprinceville.com

A "spectacular setting" with "breathtaking" ocean views, Jean-Georges Vongerichten's "brilliant" Eclectic cuisine exhibiting

"French flair with a Hawaiian accent" and "excellent" service make this Princeville resort establishment a "world-class destination" and Kauai's No. 1 for Food, Decor and Service; a "good wine list with reasonably priced options" is another plus, but some caution that "unless you have very deep pockets", save this one for "special occasions."

Kauai Pasta *Italian* 22 | 13 | 21 | $26

Kapaa | 4-939B Kuhio Hwy. (Ala Rd.) | 808-822-7447
Lihue | 3-3142 Kuhio Hwy. (Kali Rd.) | 808-245-2227
www.kauaipasta.com

"Generous portions" of "delectable" pastas, "excellent" salads and other Italian selections at "reasonable" prices are why these "cozy" siblings are among "the few bangs for your bucks in Kauai" according to fans; the "staff is family-friendly", though some feel it "needs to be more attentive", while others describe the "understated" digs as "cramped" with a "coffee-shop atmosphere."

Keoki's Paradise *Pacific Rim* 20 | 22 | 21 | $36

Poipu | Poipu Shopping Vill. | 2360 Kiahuna Plantation Dr. (Poipu Rd.) | Koloa | 808-742-7534 | www.keokisparadise.com

"Convenient to all the Poipu hotels", this scion of the "Duke's family" is geared "mainly for tourists", boasting a "tropical", "*Gilligan's Island*" setting replete with "luscious green plants, splashing waterfalls and twinkling lights" that allows you to "sightsee while never leaving your table"; ok, it might conjure up "Disneyworld", but it comes through with "well-prepared fresh fish" and other "reliable" Pacific Rim fare plus "generous" drinks, all delivered by "friendly, helpful" servers.

Kintaro 🚭 *Japanese* 24 | 18 | 21 | $40

Kapaa | 4-370 Kuhio Hwy. (Kapaa Byp.) | 808-822-3341

Some of the "freshest sushi and sashimi on the island" and teppanyaki chefs who put on a "wonderful show at the grills" are the draws at this "wildly popular" Kapaa Japanese where you can "expect a long wait" "after 6 PM"; some say the rest of the "busy" staff "needs a little help" and find the decor "nothing to speak of", but many "keep returning" for the "well-prepared", "reasonably priced" fare nonetheless.

Koloa Fish Market ⊠ ⊄ *Hawaiian/Seafood* 24 | 8 | 18 | $16

Koloa | 5482 Koloa Rd. (Kaumualii Hwy.) | 808-742-6199

There's "barely enough room to order" and "no ambiance" at this "tiny" Hawaiian-seafood "takeout-only" counter in Koloa, but "locals" "don't go for the decor", just "super-fresh fish" and "fantastic plate lunches", served up by an "efficient" staff; though some may chafe at the cash-only policy, fans argue "you can't beat the price."

Lighthouse Bistro *European/Pacific Rim* 18 | 18 | 20 | $38

Kilauea | Kong Lung Sq. | 2484 Keneke St. (Kilauea Rd.) | 808-828-0480 | www.lighthousebistro.com

"You'll love the staff" at this "underrated spot" in Kilauea serving a "solid menu" of Pacific Rim and European fusion cuisine that "provides a lot of nice options" in a "pleasant open pavilion" setting; "live music" is a plus, and while a few critics find it "overpriced" and just "ok", others deem it "worth a stop on the way to the lighthouse."

Mediterranean Gourmet ⊠ *Mediterranean* ∇ 23 | 21 | 24 | $39

Hanalei | Hanalei Colony Resort | 5-7130 Kuhio Hwy. (Alamihi Rd.) | 808-826-9875 | www.hcr.com

"Friendly" chef-owner Imad Beydoun "bounces from table to table" at his family-run Mediterranean in the Hanalei Colony Resort on Kauai's North Shore, offering "hearty", "flavorful" dishes in a room where every table has a view of the "uncrowded beach and Pacific waves"; an eclectic mix of live entertainment, from belly dancers to a "wonderful" luau that's "not the typical tourist" version, adds to its allure.

Z NEW Merriman's *Hawaii Reg.* 26 | 24 | 25 | $60

Koloa | Kukui'ula Village Mall | 2829 Ala Kalanikaumaka St. (Poipu Rd.) | 808-742-8385 | www.merrimanshawaii.com

See review in Big Island Directory.

Plantation Gardens *Pacific Rim* 23 | 25 | 23 | $48

Poipu | Outrigger Kiahuna Plantation | 2253 Poipu Rd. (Kiahuna Plantation Dr.) | Koloa | 808-742-2121 | www.pgrestaurant.com

It's like dining in "old Hawaii" when you "eat on the lanai" at this "quiet", "romantic" Pacific Rim eatery in a "spectacular" plantation locale in Poipu; though there's also "accommodating" service and a menu with just enough "flair" (don't miss the "legendary tropical drinks"), most simply "come for the atmosphere."

Pomodoro *Italian* — 17 | 14 | 20 | $36

Poipu | Rainbow Plaza, 2nd fl. | Kaumualii Hwy. (Silva Tract Rd.) | Koloa | 808-332-5945

Tucked into an "out-of-the-way", second-floor space in a "dreary" Poipu "roadside retail cluster", this "friendly", family-run restaurant fills the bill when you just "have to have Italian"; while some deem the fare "disappointing", the "huge", "cheap" portions and "welcoming" service ensure it's "always packed" with "locals and their kids."

Postcards Café *Eclectic* — 24 | 19 | 22 | $45

Hanalei | 5-5075 Kuhio Hwy. (Aku Rd.) | 808-826-1191 | www.postcardscafe.com

Set in a picture-perfect "postcard of a house", this "cozy", "low-key" Eclectic seafood and vegetarian option in Hanalei is a "must" for "super-fresh" "catches of the day", locally grown produce and "amazing" desserts (the "molten chocolate cake is worth every calorie"); they don't take reservations and it's usually "packed", but the "professional staff" "always accommodates you."

Red Salt *Hawaiian* — 26 | 23 | 24 | $58

Poipu | Koa Kea Hotel | 2251 Poipu Rd. (Hapa Rd.) | Koloa | 808-828-8888 | www.koakea.com

The "extraordinary" seafood-focused Hawaiian menu is "among the most creative" on Kauai say admirers of this "expensive" oceanside eatery in Poipu's Koa Kea Hotel, where the presentations are "artistic", the service is "superior" and the "cocktails are strong"; the "modern" decor, on the other hand, is a little "too sterile" for a handful of reviewers.

Roy's *Hawaii Reg.* — 26 | 22 | 24 | $55

Poipu | Poipu Shopping Vill. | 2360 Kiahuna Plantation Dr. (Poipu Rd.) | Koloa | 808-742-5000 | www.roysrestaurant.com

See review in Oahu Directory.

Shrimp Station *Seafood* 22 | 7 | 15 | $15

Waimea | 9652 Kaumualii Hwy. (bet. Makeke & Pokole Rds.) | 808-338-1242 | www.shrimpstation.com

Eat "like a local" at this "classic little" Kauai "roadside trailer" that's not much more than "a kitchen with picnic tables" serving "nothing but" "super-tasty", just-off-the-boat shrimp, including a coconut variety that "can't be beat"; the limited service is "excellent", and the location is perfect when "going to or coming from" "a day of hiking at Waimea Canyon" - just be sure to "get there before they sell out."

Z Tidepools *Pacific Rim/Seafood* 24 | 27 | 24 | $61

Poipu | Grand Hyatt | 1571 Poipu Rd. (bet. Ainako St. & Keleka Rd.) | Koloa | 808-742-1234 | www.kauai.hyatt.com

There's hardly a more "romantic", "postcard"-worthy setting than at this "elegant" Grand Hyatt eatery in Poipu set at "the edge of a koi pond", especially when you "ask for a waterside table"; you may "spend more time watching the thousands" of fish than focusing on the "fabulous" Pacific Rim fare, but you "can't go wrong with anything you order" and it's all brought by a "knowledgeable" staff that "knows when to dial it down for those on a date."

Tropical Taco *Mexican* ∇ 19 | 11 | 15 | $15

Hanalei | Halele'a Bldg. | 5-5088 Kuhio Hwy. (Aku Rd.) | 808-827-8226 | www.tropicaltaco.com

Loyalists love to grab a "fantastic fish taco" and "large portions" of other inexpensive Mexican fare "for lunch" on the porch of this "quick-stop" no-frills spot in Hanalei that used to operate out of a trailer (it's still parked out back); serious south-of-the-border eaters, however, dis "bland" offerings for "gullible tourists", saying you'd "never find a local eating here."

Wahoo Seafood Grill & Bar *Pacific Rim/Seafood* 22 | 19 | 22 | $41

Kapaa | 4-733 Kuhio Hwy. (Aleka Loop) | 808-822-7833 | www.wahooogrill.com

The seafood-centric Pacific Rim dishes at this Kapaa eatery (including a signature ono in a lemon-lime beurre blanc butter cream sauce) are "incredibly fresh", "creative" and "flavorful", and brought to table by a staff full of "aloha spirit"; despite a setting that a few say "lacks atmosphere", most tag it "another don't-miss."

Waimea Brewing Company *Pub Food* 17 | 18 | 19 | $26

Waimea | Waimea Plantation Cottages | 9400 Kaumualii Hwy. (Menehune Rd.) | 808-338-9733 | www.waimea-plantation.com

The local suds are "crisp on your tongue" at this brewpub in the Waimea Plantation Cottages, but reviewers are mixed on the rest: proponents like the "unique", "out-of-the-way" location, "filling" fare and "real Hawaiian musicians", while contrarians counter "such a fabulous setting deserves better" than "standard" bar grinds "with an ahi-ahi twist" and service that can be "slow as a snail."

FOOD | DECOR | SERVICE | COST

Lanai & Molokai

TOP FOOD

27 Lodge/Koele Din. Rm. | *Pac. Rim*
26 Ocean Grill | *Asian/Seafood*
24 Challenge at Manele | *Pac. Rim*
23 Hulopo'e Ct. | *Italian/Pac. Rim*
Lanai City Grille | *Hawaii Reg.*

TOP DECOR

29 Lodge/Koele Din. Rm.
26 Ocean Grill
24 Challenge at Manele
23 Hulopo'e Court
21 Lanai City Grille

TOP SERVICE

28 Lodge/Koele Din. Rm.
25 Challenge at Manele
24 Ocean Grill
Hulopo'e Court
23 Lanai City Grille

Blue Ginger Café ⊄ *American/Asian* 20 | 16 | 20 | $20

Lanai City | 409 Seventh St. (Lanai Ave.) | Lanai | 808-565-6363 | www.bluegingercafelanai.com

"Visitors and locals alike" head to this "family-style" Lanai "plate-lunch place" for "delicious, simple" American and Pan-Asian fare (aka "island food") served by "nice people" in a "casual", "hole-in-the-wall" setting; the "reasonable prices" and "homey" ambiance make it a "nice change of pace from the very upscale resort hotels."

Challenge at Manele Clubhouse *Pacific Rim* 24 | 24 | 25 | $33

Manele | Four Seasons Resort Lanai at Manele Bay | 1 Manele Bay Rd. (Manele Rd.) | Lanai City | Lanai | 808-565-2290 | www.fourseasons.com

"Breathtaking views" of the ocean and the golf course are par for this lunch spot at the Four Seasons Manele Bay, while the service and Pacific Rim fare are "exceptional for a clubhouse"; "outstanding" sandwiches and "terrific" burgers, "enjoyed outside" "with family and friends" "while watching the dolphins" - it "couldn't be better."

Hula Shores *American/Pacific Rim* - | - | - | M

Kaunakakai | Aqua Hotel Molokai | 1300 Kamehameha V Hwy. (Lahinani Pl.) | Molokai | 808-553-5347 | www.hotelmolokai.com

"Awesome views" of Lanai and a "breezy" oceanfront setting lit by tiki torches after dark make this casual, "open-air" American-

Pacific Rim specialist at the Hotel Molokai outside Kaunakakai a "fine place for drinks"; while fans recommend the "fresh fish", others shrug at the "basic" eats and insist "there are better choices locally."

Hulopo'e Court *Italian/Pacific Rim* 23 | 23 | 24 | $57

Manele | Four Seasons Resort Lanai at Manele Bay | 1 Manele Bay Rd. (Manele Rd.) | Lanai City | Lanai | 808-565-2290 | www.fourseasons.com

"You'll love the atmosphere" at the Four Seasons Manele Bay's main dining room, where "spectacular views" of the bay serve as a backdrop to dinners featuring "very professional" service and "innovative" Italian-Pacific Rim cuisine; it also serves buffet and à la carte breakfasts, and fans insist it's "worth every cent."

Kanemitsu's Bakery & Coffee Shop *Bakery* ∇ 19 | 9 | 21 | $14

Kaunakakai | 79 Ala Malama St. (bet. Hotel & Manako Lns.) | Molokai | 808-553-5855

"So Molokai", this circa-1922 Kaunakakai bakery is "famous" for its bread, but fans also praise its "super-sweet" pastries as well as local-style breakfasts and lunches, all served in a spare setting with an "at-home feeling"; devotees declare you "gotta go here once in your life."

Lanai City Grille M *Hawaii Reg.* 23 | 21 | 23 | $43

Lanai City | Hotel Lanai | 828 Lanai Ave. (9th Ave.) | Lanai | 808-565-7211 | www.hotellanai.com

Though it's housed in the Hotel Lanai, this "charming" spot has lots of "local character", serving a "creative, fresh" Hawaii Regional "menu designed by Beverly Gannon" "with aloha"; "generous portions" and a "warm", "friendly" atmosphere in the plantation-style room with "rich wood furniture" also help make it a "great change from the resorts."

Z **Lodge at Koele Dining Room** *Pacific Rim* 27 | 29 | 28 | $72

Koele | Four Seasons Lanai, The Lodge at Koele | 1 Keomoku Hwy. (Laniola Rd.) | Lanai City | Lanai | 808-565-4580 | www.fourseasons.com

Simply the "best restaurant on Lanai" according to surveyors, the "serene" dining room at the Four Seasons Koele is rated the island's

No. 1 for Food, Decor and Service thanks to "finely prepared" Euro-accented Pacific Rim cuisine served by a "top-notch" staff in a "beautiful", "grand" setting complete with a "crackling" fireplace and "clubby" ambiance; it's "pricey", to be sure, but for most it's "worth the splurge" for an "exquisite evening."

Molokai Pizza Café ⊄ *Pizza* — | — | — | I

Kaunakakai | Kahua Ctr. | 15 Kaunakakai Pl. (Kamehameha V Hwy.) | Molokai | 808-553-3288

The "only game in town for pizza" - literally - this "friendly", cash-only Kaunakakai parlor is about "more than just" pies, "also serving sandwiches and other items", while video games keep the kids busy; loyalists insist that "nothing can beat" it, but skeptics sniff you "don't go to Molokai for the food."

Ocean Grill *Asian/Seafood* 26 | 26 | 24 | $53

Manele | Four Seasons Resort Lanai at Manele Bay | 1 Manele Bay Rd. (Manele Rd.) | Lanai City | Lanai | 808-565-2092 | www.fourseasons.com

Insiders say "early evening" is the best time to head to the Four Seasons Manele Bay's seafooder, where you can "watch the sun set" over a meal of "excellent" Pan-Asian fin fare, or just "apps and drinks", in the "beautiful" open-air setting; its location is "perfect for a romantic dinner."

INDEXES

Cuisines 104
Locations 111
Special Features 118

Cuisines

Includes names, locations and Food ratings.

AMERICAN

Restaurant	Food
Beachhse. | **Waikiki/O**	23
Big City Diner | **multi.**	17
Big Island Grill | **Kailua-Kona/BI**	21
Blue Ginger | **Lanai City/L**	20
Brennecke's | **Poipu/K**	19
Bubba Burger | **multi.**	19
Bubba Gump | **multi.**	16
Cafe 100 | **Hilo/BI**	20
Charley's | **Paia/Ma**	22
Cheeseburger/Paradise | **multi.**	17
Cheesecake Fac. | **Waikiki/O**	20
Colleen's | **Haiku/Ma**	21
Contemp. Café | **Makiki Hts/O**	21
Dollie's Pub | **Lahaina/Ma**	19
Downtown/HISAM | **Downtown/O**	24
Duane's Ono-Char | **Anahola/K**	24
Duke's | **multi.**	20
Eggs 'n Things | **Waikiki/O**	22
Gazebo | **Napili/Ma**	24
Hanalei Gourmet | **Hanalei/K**	21
Hard Rock | **multi.**	15
Hula Shores | **Kaunakakai/Mo**	-
Island Burger | **Ala Moana/O**	19
Jimmy Buffett's | **Waikiki/O**	18
Joe's B&G | **Wailea/Ma**	21
Kihei Caffe | **Kihei/Ma**	25
Kimo's | **Lahaina/Ma**	21
Kona Brewing | **multi.**	20
Kula Lodge | **Kula/Ma**	21
Lahaina Grill | **Lahaina/Ma**	26
MAC 24/7 | **Waikiki/O**	19
Manago | **Captain Cook/BI**	21
Mariposa | **Ala Moana/O**	23
Monettes | **Kohala/BI**	24
Oceanarium | **Waikiki/O**	17
'Ono Bar & Grill | **Kaanapali/Ma**	19
Original Pancake | **multi.**	21
Prince Ct. | **Waikiki/O**	22
Quinn's | **Kailua-Kona/BI**	21
Ruby's | **Kahului/Ma**	20
Shore Bird | **Waikiki/O**	16
Side St. Inn | **multi.**	24
Stage | **Ala Moana/O**	22
Stella Blues | **Kihei/Ma**	20
Tangö | **Downtown/O**	24
Town | **Kaimuki/O**	24
12th Ave. | **Kaimuki/O**	24
Uncle's Fish | **Iwilei/O**	21
Willows | **Moiliili/O**	18

ASIAN

Restaurant	Food
Blue Ginger | **Lanai City/L**	20
Daniel Thiebaut | **Waimea/BI**	24
Indigo | **Chinatown/O**	21
I'O | **Lahaina/Ma**	25
Ocean Grill | **Manele/L**	26
Spices | **Moiliili/O**	24
Stage | **Ala Moana/O**	22
Tommy Bahama's | **multi.**	21
Wild Ginger | **Kaimuki/O**	21

BAKERIES

Restaurant	Food
Hanapepe Café | **Hanapepe/K**	22
Kalaheo Café | **Kalaheo/K**	23
Kanemitsu's | **Kaunakakai/Mo**	19
Panya | **Downtown/O**	21

BARBECUE

Restaurant	Food
Tony Roma | **multi.**	19

CUISINES

BURGERS

Bubba Burger | **multi.** 19
Burgers/Edge | **Kapahulu/O** 17
Cheeseburger/Paradise | **multi.** 17
Duane's Ono-Char | **Anahola/K** 24
Hard Rock | **multi.** 15
Island Burger | **Ala Moana/O** 19
Jimmy Buffett's | **Waikiki/O** 18
Kua 'Aina | **multi.** 22
Peggy Sue's | **Kihei/Ma** 21

CALIFORNIAN

Beach Tree | **Kaupulehu-Kona/BI** 24
Z Spago | **Wailea/Ma** 26

CARIBBEAN

Tommy Bahama's | **multi.** 21

CHINESE

(* dim sum specialist)
Ciao Mein | **Waikiki/O** 22
Dragon Dragon | **Kahului/Ma** 19
Fook Yuen | **McCully/O** 22
Kirin* | **Moiliili/O** 23
Little Village | **Chinatown/O** 23
Pah Ke's | **Kaneohe/O** 22
P.F. Chang's | **multi.** 19

COFFEEHOUSES

Kalaheo Café | **Kalaheo/K** 23

COFFEE SHOPS/ DINERS

Highway Inn | **Waipahu/O** 21
MAC 24/7 | **Waikiki/O** 19
Original Pancake | **multi.** 21
Paniolo Inn | **Kamuela/BI** 20
Peggy Sue's | **Kihei/Ma** 21
Ruby's | **Kahului/Ma** 20

CONTINENTAL

Castaway | **Kaanapali/Ma** 21

DESSERT

Cheesecake Fac. | **Waikiki/O** 20
Kincaid's | **Ward/O** 20
Z Matsumoto's | **Haleiwa/O** 23

ECLECTIC

Banyan Tree | **Kapalua/Ma** 24
Café Pesto | **multi.** 23
Z CanoeHouse | **Kohala/BI** 24
Casa di Amici | **Poipu/K** 23
Hanalei Gourmet | **Hanalei/K** 21
Jackie Rey's | **Kailua-Kona/BI** 24
Z NEW Kauai Grill | **Princeville/K** 26
Keei Café | **Kealakekua/BI** 24
Kilauea Lodge | **Volcano/BI** 21
Lahaina Coolers | **Lahaina/Ma** 19
Lucy's Grill | **Kailua/O** 21
Pagoda | **Ala Moana/O** 17
Paniolo Inn | **Kamuela/BI** 20
Postcards | **Hanalei/K** 24

EURASIAN

Z Hiroshi | **Restaurant Row/O** 28

EUROPEAN FUSION

Lighthouse | **Kilauea/K** 18

FRENCH

Z Chef Mavro | **Moiliili/O** 27
Duc's Bistro | **Chinatown/O** 24
Formaggio | **multi.** 21
Z Gerard's | **Lahaina/Ma** 26
Hale Samoa | **Kailua-Kona/BI** 20
La Bourgogne | **Kailua-Kona/BI** 26
Z La Mer | **Waikiki/O** 28
Z Le Bistro | **Niu Valley/O** 27
Z Michel's | **Waikiki/O** 27

Monettes | **Kohala/BI** 24
Panya | **Ala Moana/O** 21

FRENCH (BISTRO)

Panya | **multi.** 21

FRENCH (BRASSERIE)

Brasserie/Vin | **Chinatown/O** 22

GREEK

Fat Greek | **Kaimuki/O** 17
Olive Tree | **Kahala/O** 25

HAWAIIAN

Aloha Mix Plate | **Lahaina/Ma** 21
Cafe 100 | **Hilo/BI** 20
Cafe O'Lei | **multi.** 24
NEW Cane & Taro | **Kaanapali/Ma** 19
David Paul's | **Lahaina/Ma** 26
Helena's | **Kalihi/O** 25
Highway Inn | **Waipahu/O** 21
Kaka'ako | **Ward/O** 22
Koloa Fish | **Koloa/K** 24
Manago | **Captain Cook/BI** 21
'Ono Bar & Grill | **Kaanapali/Ma** 19
Ono Hawaii | **Kapahulu/O** 25
Red Salt | **Poipu/K** 26
Willows | **Moiliili/O** 18

HAWAII REGIONAL

Z Alan Wong's | **McCully/O** 28
Z Chef Mavro | **Moiliili/O** 27
Daniel Thiebaut | **Waimea/BI** 24
Gannon's | **Wailea/Ma** 23
Z Hali'imaile Gen. | **Makawao/Ma** 27
Lanai City | **Lanai City/L** 23
Mala | **multi.** 25
Manta/Pavilion | **Kohala/BI** 25
Z Merriman's | **multi.** 26
NEW Monstera | **Kohala/BI** -
Ola | **Kahuku/O** 21
Z Pahu i'a | **Kaupulehu-Kona/BI** 26
Pineapple Rm. | **Ala Moana/O** 24
Z Roy's | **multi.** 26
Sam Choy's | **Iwilei/O** 19
Umalu | **Kaanapali/Ma** 22

ITALIAN

(N=Northern; S=Southern)

Arancino | **Waikiki/O** 24
Aroma D'Italia | S | **Kihei/Ma** 19
Assaggio | **multi.** 21
Auntie Pasto | **multi.** 19
Baci Bistro | **Kailua/O** 25
Beach Tree | **Kaupulehu-Kona/BI** 24
Casanova | N | **multi.** 20
Café Portofino | N | **Kalapaki Bch/K** 22
Cafe Sistina | N | **Makiki/O** 21
Capische? | N | **Wailea/Ma** 25
Casa di Amici | **Poipu/K** 23
Ciao Mein | **Waikiki/O** 22
Z Dondero's | N | **Poipu/K** 25
Ferraro's | **Wailea/Ma** 24
Hulopo'e Ct. | **Manele/L** 23
Kauai Pasta | **multi.** 22
Longhi's | **multi.** 21
Matteo's | **Wailea/Ma** 21
Mediterraneo | **Makiki/O** 24
Mix Café | **Downtown/O** 21
Paesano | **multi.** 20
Penne Pasta | **Lahaina/Ma** 20
Pomodoro | **Poipu/K** 17
Romano's | **multi.** 17
Sarento's Top | **Waikiki/O** 19
Sergio's | **Waikiki/O** 18
Taormina | S | **Waikiki/O** 25
Tavola | N | **Diamond Head/O** 22

Town | **Kaimuki/O** 24
Verbano | S | **multi.** 19
Vino | **Restaurant Row/O** 24

JAPANESE

(* sushi specialist)

Akasaka* | **Ala Moana/O** 24
Benihana | **Waikiki/O** 19
California Bch.* | **Ward/O** 20
Ezogiku | **multi.** 21
Genki Sushi* | **multi.** 16
Goma Tei | **multi.** 22
Gyotaku | **multi.** 20
Hakkei | **Makiki/O** 26
Hakone* | **Waikiki/O** 26
Hanamaulu Cafe* | **Lihue/K** 22
Ichiriki Nabe | **Ala Moana/O** 24
Imari* | **Kohala/BI** 22
Kenichi* | **Keauhou/BI** 24
Kintaro* | **Kapaa/K** 24
Kobe/Oku's* | **multi.** 22
Kozo Sushi* | **multi.** 20
NEW Monstera | **Kohala/BI** -
NEW Morimoto | **Waikiki/O** -
Z Nobu* | **Waikiki/O** 27
Norio's* | **Kohala/BI** 24
Okonomiyaki | **Waikiki/O** 21
Panya | **multi.** 21
Rokkaku | **Ala Moana/O** 24
Z Sansei* | **multi.** 25
Shirokiya* | **Ala Moana/O** 21
Shokudo | **Ala Moana/O** 22
Suntory* | **Waikiki/O** 23
Sushi King* | **Moiliili/O** 19
Z Sushi Sasabune* | **Ala Moana/O** 28
Tanaka | **multi.** 21
Tanioka's | **Waipahu/O** 24
Teshima's | **Kealakekua/BI** 20
Tokyo Tei | **Wailuku/Ma** 20
Tsukuneya | **University/O** 20
Yanagi* | **Kakaako/O** 23
Yohei* | **Kapalama/O** 25

KOREAN

(* barbecue specialist)

Isana* | **Kihei/Ma** 27
Sorabol* | **Ala Moana/O** 22

MALAYSIAN

Green Door | **Chinatown/O** 22

MEDITERRANEAN

Bar Acuda | **Hanalei/K** 25
Casanova | **Kahului/Ma** 20
Casablanca | **Poipu/K** 18
Formaggio | **multi.** 21
Kiawe Kitchen | **Volcano/BI** 23
Market Fresh | **Makawao/Ma** -
Med. Gourmet | **Hanalei/K** 23
Merriman's Café | **Waikoloa/BI** 21
Pavilion Café | **Ala Moana/O** 24
Plantation Hse. | **Kapalua/Ma** 25
Sarento's/Bch. | **Kihei/Ma** 25

MEXICAN

Cholo's | **Haleiwa/O** 16
Cilantro Grill | **Lahaina/Ma** 23
Maui Tacos | **multi.** 19
Milagros | **Paia/Ma** 20
Tropical Taco | **Hanalei/K** 19
Wahoo's Fish | **Ward/O** 18

NOODLE SHOPS

Ezogiku | **multi.** 21
Goma Tei | **multi.** 22

NORTH AFRICAN

Casablanca | **Poipu/K** 18

PACIFIC RIM

Bali Steaks/Seafood | **Waikiki/O** 24

Bamboo | **Hawi/BI** 23

Z Beach Hse. | **Poipu/K** 24

Chai's Is. | **Downtown/O** 25

Challenge/Manele | **Manele/L** 24

Coast Grille | **Kohala/BI** 21

Don/Beachcomber | **Kailua-Kona/BI** 17

NEW Duke's Beach Hse. | **Kaanapali/Ma** 21

Five Palms | **Kihei/Ma** 21

Hale Samoa | **Kailua-Kona/BI** 20

Hau Tree | **Waikiki/O** 21

Hilo Bay Café | **Hilo/BI** 26

Hoku's | **Kahala/O** 26

Huggos | **Kailua-Kona/BI** 21

Hula Grill | **multi.** 21

Hula Shores | **Kaunakakai/Mo** -

Hulopo'e Ct. | **Manele/L** 23

Humuhumunukunukuapua'a | **Wailea/Ma** 22

Kamuela Provision | **Kohala/BI** 21

Keoki's Paradise | **Poipu/K** 20

Kiawe Kitchen | **Volcano/BI** 23

Lighthouse | **Kilauea/K** 18

Z Lodge/Koele | **Koele/L** 27

Z Mama's Fish | **Paia/Ma** 27

Ocean Hse. | **Waikiki/O** 24

Z Orchids | **Waikiki/O** 26

Pacific'O | **Lahaina/Ma** 25

Pineapple Grill | **Kapalua/Ma** 25

Plantation Gdns. | **Poipu/K** 23

Prince Ct. | **Waikiki/O** 22

RumFire | **Waikiki/O** 20

Z Sansei | **multi.** 25

Sea House | **Napili/Ma** 22

Z Spago | **Wailea/Ma** 26

3660/Rise | **Kaimuki/O** 25

Z Tidepools | **Poipu/K** 24

Tiki's Grill | **Waikiki/O** 17

21 Degrees North | **Kahuku/O** 21

Wahoo Seafood | **Kapaa/K** 22

PERUVIAN

Z Nobu | **Waikiki/O** 27

PIZZA

Antonio's | **multi.** 19

California Pizza | **multi.** 20

Dollie's Pub | **Lahaina/Ma** 19

Flatbread | **Paia/Ma** 25

Kula Lodge | **Kula/Ma** 21

Matteo's | **Wailea/Ma** 21

Molokai Pizza | **Kaunakakai/Mo** -

Round Table | **multi.** 19

POLYNESIAN

Feast at Lele | **Lahaina/Ma** 23

PUB FOOD

Dollie's Pub | **Lahaina/Ma** 19

Kona Brewing | **multi.** 20

Waimea Brew | **Waimea/K** 17

SANDWICHES

Kua 'Aina | **multi.** 22

Mix Café | **Downtown/O** 21

Molokai Pizza | **Kaunakakai/Mo** -

SEAFOOD

Azure | **Waikiki/O** 25

Brennecke's | **Poipu/K** 19

Brown's Bch. | **Kohala/BI** 24

Bubba Gump | **multi.** 16

Buzz's Wharf | **Maalaea/Ma** 20

Cafe O'Lei | **multi.** 24

Duo | **Wailea/Ma** 25

Five Palms | **Kihei/Ma** 21

Hanalei Dolphin | **Hanalei/K** 23

Hau Tree | **Waikiki/O** 21
Huggos | **Kailua-Kona/BI** 21
Hula Grill | **multi.** 21
Jameson's | **Haleiwa/O** 19
Kamuela Provision | **Kohala/BI** 21
Kimo's | **Lahaina/Ma** 21
Kincaid's | **Ward/O** 20
Koloa Fish | **Koloa/K** 24
Kona Inn | **Kailua-Kona/BI** 20
Leilani's | **Kaanapali/Ma** 20
Longhi's | **multi.** 21
Mala | **multi.** 25
Z Mama's Fish | **Paia/Ma** 27
Z Merriman's | **Poipu/K** 26
Nick's Fishmkt. | **Wailea/Ma** 23
Nico's/Pier 38 | **Iwilei/O** 25
Oceanarium | **Waikiki/O** 17
Ocean Grill | **Manele/L** 26
Ocean Hse. | **Waikiki/O** 24
Z Orchids | **Waikiki/O** 26
Pacific'O | **Lahaina/Ma** 25
Z Pahu i'a | **Kaupulehu-Kona/BI** 26
Paia Fish Mkt. | **Paia/Ma** 26
Postcards | **Hanalei/K** 24
Quinn's | **Kailua-Kona/BI** 21
Z Sansei | **multi.** 25
Shrimp Sta. | **Waimea/K** 22
Z Son'z | **Kaanapali/Ma** 24
Tanioka's | **Waipahu/O** 24
3660/Rise | **Kaimuki/O** 25
Z Tidepools | **Poipu/K** 24
21 Degrees North | **Kahuku/O** 21
Uncle's Fish | **Iwilei/O** 21
Wahoo Seafood | **Kapaa/K** 22
Waterfront Rest. | **Maalaea/Ma** 25

SINGAPOREAN

Green Door | **Chinatown/O** 22

SMALL PLATES

Bar Acuda | Med. | **Hanalei/K** 25
Casanova | Italian/Med. | **Kahului/Ma** 20
Brasserie/Vin | French | **Chinatown/O** 22
Formaggio | Med. | **Kaimuki/O** 21
Z Hiroshi | Eurasian | **Restaurant Row/O** 28
Huggos | Pac. Rim | **Kailua-Kona/BI** 21
RumFire | Pac. Rim | **Waikiki/O** 20
Vino | Italian | **Restaurant Row/O** 24

STEAKHOUSES

Beachhse. | **Waikiki/O** 23
NEW BLT Steak | **Waikiki/O** 24
Bull Shed | **Kapaa/K** 22
Buzz's | **multi.** 20
Buzz's Wharf | **Maalaea/Ma** 20
Cafe O'Lei | **multi.** 24
DK Steak House | **Waikiki/O** 22
Duo | **Wailea/Ma** 25
Hy's Steak | **Waikiki/O** 26
Jameson's | **Haleiwa/O** 19
Kamuela Provision | **Kohala/BI** 21
Kincaid's | **Ward/O** 20
Kobe/Oku's | **multi.** 22
Leilani's | **Kaanapali/Ma** 20
Makawao Steak | **Makawao/Ma** 20
Morton's | **Ala Moana/O** 24
Outback | **multi.** 18
Ruth's Chris | **multi.** 25
Z Son'z | **Kaanapali/Ma** 24
Wolfgang's Steak | **Waikiki/O** 24

THAI

Chiang Mai Thai | **Moiliili/O** 20
Haleiwa Eats Thai | **Haleiwa/O** 24
Keo's | **Waikiki/O** 22

Mekong Thai | **Ala Moana/O** 21

Phuket Thai | **multi.** 23

Singha Thai | **Waikiki/O** 21

VEGETARIAN

(* vegan)

Hanapepe Café* | **Hanapepe/K** 22

Postcards | **Hanalei/K** 24

Stella Blues* | **Kihei/Ma** 20

VIETNAMESE

A Saigon Café | **Wailuku/Ma** 23

Bac Nam | **Downtown/O** 23

Duc's Bistro | **Chinatown/O** 24

Hale Vietnam | **Kaimuki/O** 22

Vietnam/Pho | **Chinatown/O** 25

Locations

Includes names, cuisines and Food ratings.

Oahu

AIEA

- Big City Diner | *Amer.* 17
- California Pizza | *Pizza* 20
- Ezogiku | *Japanese/Noodles* 21
- Kozo Sushi | *Japanese* 20
- Paesano | *Italian* 20
- Tony Roma | *BBQ* 19
- Verbano | *Italian* 19

ALA MOANA

- Akasaka | *Japanese* 24
- Assaggio | *Italian* 21
- Bubba Gump | *Amer./Seafood* 16
- California Pizza | *Pizza* 20
- Genki Sushi | *Japanese* 16
- Goma Tei | *Japanese/Noodles* 22
- Ichiriki Nabe | *Japanese* 24
- Island Burger | *Burgers* 19
- Longhi's | *Italian* 21
- Mariposa | *Amer.* 23
- Mekong Thai | *Thai* 21
- Morton's | *Steak* 24
- Original Pancake | *Amer.* 21
- Pagoda | *Eclectic* 17
- Panya | *French/Japanese* 21
- Pavilion Café | *Med.* 24
- P.F. Chang's | *Chinese* 19
- Pineapple Rm. | *Hawaii Reg.* 24
- Rokkaku | *Japanese* 24
- Romano's | *Italian* 17
- Shirokiya | *Japanese* 21
- Shokudo | *Japanese* 22
- Side St. Inn | *Amer.* 24
- Sorabol | *Korean* 22
- Stage | *Amer./Asian* 22
- Z Sushi Sasabune | *Japanese* 28
- Tanaka | *Japanese* 21

CHINATOWN

- Brasserie/Vin | *French* 22
- Duc's Bistro | *French/Viet.* 24
- Green Door | *Malaysian/Singaporean* 22
- Indigo | *Asian* 21
- Little Village | *Chinese* 23
- Vietnam/Pho | *Viet.* 25

DIAMOND HEAD

- Tavola | *Italian* 22

DOWNTOWN

- Auntie Pasto | *Italian* 19
- Bac Nam | *Viet.* 23
- Chai's Is. | *Pac. Rim* 25
- Downtown/HISAM | *Amer.* 24
- Gyotaku | *Japanese* 20
- Mix Café | *Italian/Sandwiches* 21
- Panya | *French/Japanese* 21
- Tangö | *Amer.* 24

EWA BEACH

- Genki Sushi | *Japanese* 16

HALEIWA

- Cholo's | *Mex.* 16
- Haleiwa Eats Thai | *Thai* 24
- Jameson's | *Seafood/Steak* 19
- Kua 'Aina | *Burgers/Sandwiches* 22
- Z Matsumoto's | *Dessert* 23

HAWAII KAI

Assaggio | *Italian* 21
Kona Brewing | *Amer.* 20
Outback | *Steak* 18
Z Roy's | *Hawaii Reg.* 26

IWILEI

Nico's/Pier 38 | *Seafood* 25
Sam Choy's | *Hawaii Reg.* 19
Uncle's Fish | *Seafood* 21

KAHALA

Antonio's | *Pizza* 19
Assaggio | *Italian* 21
Hoku's | *Pac. Rim* 26
Kozo Sushi | *Japanese* 20
Olive Tree | *Greek* 25

KAHUKU

Ola | *Hawaii Reg.* 21
21 Degrees North | *Seafood* 21

KAILUA

Assaggio | *Italian* 21
Baci Bistro | *Italian* 25
Big City Diner | *Amer.* 17
California Pizza | *Pizza* 20
Formaggio | *Med.* 21
Lucy's Grill | *Eclectic* 21
Maui Tacos | *Mexican* 19
Round Table | *Pizza* 19

KAIMUKI

Big City Diner | *Amer.* 17
Fat Greek | *Greek* 17
Formaggio | *Med.* 21
Hale Vietnam | *Viet.* 22
3660/Rise | *Pac. Rim* 25
Town | *Amer./Italian* 24
12th Ave. | *Amer.* 24
Verbano | *Italian* 19
Wild Ginger | *Asian* 21

KAKAAKO

Yanagi | *Japanese* 23

KALIHI

Helena's | *Hawaiian* 25

KANEOHE

Genki Sushi | *Japanese* 16
Pah Ke's | *Chinese* 22

KAPAHULU

Burgers/Edge | *Burgers* 17
Genki Sushi | *Japanese* 16
Kozo Sushi | *Japanese* 20
Ono Hawaii | *Hawaiian* 25
Side St. Inn | *Amer.* 24

KAPALAMA

Original Pancake | *Amer.* 21
Yohei | *Japanese* 25

KAPOLEI

Assaggio | *Italian* 21
Outback | *Steak* 18
Z Roy's | *Hawaii Reg.* 26

LANIKAI

Buzz's | *Steak* 20

MAKIKI

Cafe Sistina | *Italian* 21
Hakkei | *Japanese* 26
Mediterraneo | *Italian* 24

MAKIKI HEIGHTS

Contemp. Café | *Amer.* 21

MANOA

Paesano | *Italian* 20

MCCULLY

- Z Alan Wong's | *Hawaii Reg.* 28
- Fook Yuen | *Chinese* 22
- Phuket Thai | *Thai* 23

MILILANI

- Assaggio | *Italian* 21
- Phuket Thai | *Thai* 23

MOILIILI

- Z Chef Mavro | *French/Hawaii Reg.* 27
- Chiang Mai Thai | *Thai* 20
- Kirin | *Chinese* 23
- Kozo Sushi | *Japanese* 20
- Spices | *Asian* 24
- Sushi King | *Japanese* 19
- Willows | *Amer./Hawaiian* 18

NIU VALLEY

- Gyotaku | *Japanese* 20
- Z Le Bistro | *French* 27

PEARL CITY

- Antonio's | *Pizza* 19
- Buzz's | *Steak* 20
- Ezogiku | *Japanese/Noodles* 21
- Genki Sushi | *Japanese* 16
- Gyotaku | *Japanese* 20
- Kozo Sushi | *Japanese* 20

RESTAURANT ROW

- Z Hiroshi | *Eurasian* 28
- Ruth's Chris | *Steak* 25
- Vino | *Italian* 24

UNIVERSITY

- Ezogiku | *Japanese/Noodles* 21
- Tsukuneya | *Japanese* 20

WAIKIKI

- Arancino | *Italian* 24
- Azure | *Seafood* 25
- Bali Steaks/Seafood | *Pac. Rim* 24
- Beachhse. | *Amer./Steak* 23
- Benihana | *Japanese* 19
- NEW BLT Steak | *Steak* 24
- California Pizza | *Pizza* 20
- Cheeseburger/Paradise | *Amer.* 17
- Cheesecake Fac. | *Amer.* 20
- Ciao Mein | *Chinese/Italian* 22
- DK Steak House | *Steak* 22
- Duke's | *Amer.* 20
- Eggs 'n Things | *Amer.* 22
- Ezogiku | *Japanese/Noodles* 21
- Hakone | *Japanese* 26
- Hard Rock | *Amer.* 15
- Hau Tree | *Pac. Rim* 21
- Hula Grill | *Pac. Rim* 21
- Hy's Steak | *Steak* 26
- Jimmy Buffett's | *Amer.* 18
- Keo's | *Thai* 22
- Kobe/Oku's | *Japanese* 22
- Z La Mer | *French* 28
- MAC 24/7 | *Amer.* 19
- Maui Tacos | *Mexican* 19
- Z Michel's | *French* 27
- NEW Morimoto | *Japanese* -
- Z Nobu | *Japanese/Peru* 27
- Oceanarium | *Amer./Seafood* 17
- Ocean Hse. | *Pac. Rim/Seafood* 24
- Okonomiyaki | *Japanese* 21
- Z Orchids | *Pac. Rim* 26
- Outback | *Steak* 18
- Panya | *French/Japanese* 21
- P.F. Chang's | *Chinese* 19
- Prince Ct. | *Amer./Pac. Rim* 22
- Round Table | *Pizza* 19
- Z Roy's | *Hawaii Reg.* 26
- RumFire | *Pac. Rim* 20
- Ruth's Chris | *Steak* 25
- Z Sansei | *Japanese/Pac. Rim* 25

Sarento's Top | *Italian* 19
Sergio's | *Italian* 18
Shore Bird | *Amer.* 16
Singha Thai | *Thai* 21
Suntory | *Japanese* 23
Tanaka | *Japanese* 21
Taormina | *Italian* 25
Tiki's Grill | *Pac. Rim* 17
Tony Roma | *BBQ* 19
Verbano | *Italian* 19
Wolfgang's Steak | *Steak* 24

WAIPAHU

Auntie Pasto | *Italian* 19
Big City Diner | *Amer.* 17
Genki Sushi | *Japanese* 16
Highway Inn | *Diner* 21
Outback | *Steak* 18
Tanioka's | *Japanese/Seafood* 24

WARD

Big City Diner | *Amer.* 17
California Bch. | *Japanese* 20
Genki Sushi | *Japanese* 16
Goma Tei | *Japanese/Noodles* 22
Kaka'ako | *Hawaiian* 22
Kincaid's | *Seafood/Steak* 20
Kua 'Aina | *Burgers/Sandwiches* 22
Phuket Thai | *Thai* 23
Wahoo's Fish | *Mex.* 18

Maui

HAIKU

Colleen's | *Amer.* 21

KAANAPALI

NEW Cane & Taro | *Hawaiian* 19
Castaway | *Continental* 21
NEW Duke's Beach Hse. | *Pac. Rim* 21
Hula Grill | *Pac. Rim* 21
Leilani's | *Seafood/Steak* 20
'Ono Bar & Grill | *Amer./Hawaiian* 19
Round Table | *Pizza* 19
Z Son'z | *Seafood/Steak* 24
Umalu | *Hawaii Reg.* 22

KAHULUI

Casanova | *Italian* 20
Cafe O'Lei | *Seafood/Steak* 24
California Pizza | *Pizza* 20
Dragon Dragon | *Chinese* 19
Genki Sushi | *Japanese* 16
Maui Tacos | *Mexican* 19
Ruby's | *Diner* 20

KAPALUA

Banyan Tree | *Eclectic* 24
Z Merriman's | *Hawaii Reg.* 26
Pineapple Grill | *Pac. Rim* 25
Plantation Hse. | *Med.* 25
Z Sansei | *Japanese/Pac. Rim* 25

KIHEI

Aroma D'Italia | *Italian* 19
Cafe O'Lei | *Seafood/Steak* 24
Cheeseburger/Paradise | *Amer.* 17
Five Palms | *Pac. Rim/Seafood* 21
Isana | *Korean* 27
Kihei Caffe | *Amer.* 25
Maui Tacos | *Mexican* 19
Outback | *Steak* 18
Peggy Sue's | *Diner* 21
Round Table | *Pizza* 19
Z Sansei | *Japanese/Pac. Rim* 25
Sarento's/Bch. | *Med.* 25
Stella Blues | *Amer.* 20

KULA

Kula Lodge | *Amer.* 21

LAHAINA

Aloha Mix Plate | *Hawaiian*	21
Bubba Gump | *Amer./Seafood*	16
Cheeseburger/Paradise | *Amer.*	17
Cilantro Grill | *Mex.*	23
David Paul's | *Hawaiian*	26
Dollie's Pub | *Pub*	19
Feast at Lele | *Polynesian*	23
Genki Sushi | *Japanese*	16
Z Gerard's | *French*	26
Hard Rock | *Amer.*	15
I'O | *Asian*	25
Kimo's | *Amer./Seafood*	21
Kobe/Oku's | *Japanese*	22
Lahaina Coolers | *Eclectic*	19
Lahaina Grill | *Amer.*	26
Longhi's | *Italian*	21
Mala | *Hawaii Reg./Seafood*	25
Maui Tacos | *Mexican*	19
Outback | *Steak*	18
Pacific'O | *Pac. Rim/Seafood*	25
Penne Pasta | *Italian*	20
Z Roy's | *Hawaii Reg.*	26
Ruth's Chris | *Steak*	25

MAALAEA

Buzz's Wharf | *Seafood/Steak*	20
Waterfront Rest. | *Seafood*	25

MAKAWAO

Casanova | *Italian*	20
Z Hali'imaile Gen. | *Hawaii Reg.*	27
Makawao Steak | *Steak*	20
Market Fresh | *Med.*	-

NAPILI

Cafe O'Lei | *Seafood/Steak*	24
Gazebo | *Amer.*	24
Maui Tacos | *Mexican*	19
Sea House | *Pac. Rim*	22

PAIA

Charley's | *Amer.*	22
Flatbread | *Pizza*	25
Z Mama's Fish | *Seafood*	27
Milagros | *Mex.*	20
Paia Fish Mkt. | *Seafood*	26

WAILEA

Capische? | *Italian*	25
Duo | *Seafood/Steak*	25
Ferraro's | *Italian*	24
Gannon's | *Hawaii Reg.*	23
Humuhumunukunukuapua'a | *Pac. Rim*	22
Joe's B&G | *Amer.*	21
Longhi's | *Italian*	21
Mala | *Hawaii Reg./Seafood*	25
Matteo's | *Italian*	21
Nick's Fishmkt. | *Seafood*	23
Ruth's Chris | *Steak*	25
Z Spago | *Cal./Pac. Rim*	26
Tommy Bahama's | *Asian/Carib.*	21

WAILUKU

A Saigon Café | *Viet.*	23
Cafe O'Lei | *Seafood/Steak*	24
Tokyo Tei | *Japanese*	20

Big Island

CAPTAIN COOK

Manago | *Amer./Hawaiian*	21

HAWI

Bamboo | *Pac. Rim*	23

HILO

Cafe 100 | *Amer./Hawaiian*	20
Café Pesto | *Eclectic*	23
Hilo Bay Café | *Pac. Rim*	26
Maui Tacos | *Mexican*	19

KAILUA-KONA

Big Island Grill | *Amer.* 21

Bubba Gump | *Amer./Seafood* 16

Don/Beachcomber | *Pac. Rim* 17

Hale Samoa | *French/Pac. Rim* 20

Huggos | *Pac. Rim/Seafood* 21

Jackie Rey's | *Eclectic* 24

Kona Brewing | *Amer.* 20

Kona Inn | *Seafood* 20

La Bourgogne | *French* 26

Outback | *Steak* 18

Quinn's | *Seafood* 21

KAMUELA

Paniolo Inn | *Eclectic* 20

KAUPULEHU-KONA

Beach Tree | *Cal./Italian* 24

Z Pahu i'a | *Hawaii Reg./Seafood* 26

KAWAIHAE HARBOR

Café Pesto | *Eclectic* 23

KEALAKEKUA

Keei Café | *Eclectic* 24

Teshima's | *Japanese* 20

KEAUHOU

Kenichi | *Asian/Japanese* 24

KOHALA COAST

Brown's Bch. | *Seafood* 24

Z CanoeHouse | *Eclectic* 24

Coast Grille | *Pac. Rim* 21

Imari | *Japanese* 22

Kamuela Provision | *Pac. Rim* 21

Manta/Pavilion | *Hawaii Reg.* 25

Monettes | *Amer./French* 24

NEW Monstera | *Japanese/Hawaii Reg.* -

Norio's | *Japanese* 24

Ruth's Chris | *Steak* 25

Z Sansei | *Japanese/Pac. Rim* 25

Tommy Bahama's | *Asian/Carib.* 21

VOLCANO

Kiawe Kitchen | *Med./Pac. Rim* 23

Kilauea Lodge | *Eclectic* 21

WAIKOLOA

Buzz's | *Steak* 20

Merriman's Café | *Med.* 21

Romano's | *Italian* 17

Z Roy's | *Hawaii Reg.* 26

WAIMEA

Daniel Thiebaut | *Asian/Hawaii Reg.* 24

Z Merriman's | *Hawaii Reg.* 26

Kauai

ANAHOLA

Duane's Ono-Char | *Burgers* 24

HANALEI

Bar Acuda | *Med.* 25

Bubba Burger | *Burgers* 19

Hanalei Dolphin | *Seafood* 23

Hanalei Gourmet | *Amer./Eclectic* 21

Med. Gourmet | *Med.* 23

Postcards | *Eclectic* 24

Tropical Taco | *Mex.* 19

HANAPEPE

Hanapepe Café | *Bakery/Veg.* 22

KALAHEO

Kalaheo Café | *Coffee* 23

KALAPAKI BEACH

Café Portofino | *Italian* 22

Duke's | *Amer.* 20

KAPAA

Bubba Burger | *Burgers* 19
Bull Shed | *Steak* 22
Kauai Pasta | *Italian* 22
Kintaro | *Japanese* 24
Wahoo Seafood | *Pac. Rim/Seafood* 22

KILAUEA

Lighthouse | *Euro./Pac. Rim* 18

KOLOA

Bubba Burger | *Burgers* 19
Koloa Fish | *Hawaiian/Seafood* 24

LIHUE

Genki Sushi | *Japanese* 16
Hanamaulu Cafe | *Japanese/Tea* 22
Kauai Pasta | *Italian* 22

POIPU

Z Beach Hse. | *Pac. Rim* 24
Brennecke's | *Amer./Seafood* 19
Casablanca | *African/Med.* 18
Casa di Amici | *Eclectic/Italian* 23
Z Dondero's | *Italian* 25
Keoki's Paradise | *Pac. Rim* 20
Z Merriman's | *Hawaii Reg.* 26
Plantation Gdns. | *Pac. Rim* 23
Pomodoro | *Italian* 17

Red Salt | *Hawaiian* 26
Z Roy's | *Hawaii Reg.* 26
Z Tidepools | *Pac. Rim/Seafood* 24

PRINCEVILLE

Z NEW Kauai Grill | *Eclectic* 26

WAIMEA

Shrimp Sta. | *Seafood* 22
Waimea Brew | *Pub* 17

Lanai & Molokai

KAUNAKAKAI

Hula Shores | *Amer./Pac. Rim* -
Kanemitsu's | *Bakery* 19
Molokai Pizza | *Pizza* -

KOELE

Z Lodge/Koele | *Pac. Rim* 27

LANAI CITY

Blue Ginger | *Amer./Asian* 20
Lanai City | *Hawaii Reg.* 23

MANELE

Challenge/Manele | *Pac. Rim* 24
Hulopo'e Ct. | *Italian/Pac. Rim* 23
Ocean Grill | *Asian/Seafood* 26

Special Features

Listings cover the best in each category and include names, locations and Food ratings. Multi-location restaurants' features may vary by branch.

BREAKFAST

Big City Diner | **multi.** 17
Blue Ginger | **Lanai City/L** 20
Cafe 100 | **Hilo/BI** 20
Eggs 'n Things | **Waikiki/O** 22
Kihei Caffe | **Kihei/Ma** 25
Original Pancake | **multi.** 21
Paniolo Inn | **Kamuela/BI** 20
Ruby's | **Kahului/Ma** 20
Sam Choy's | **Iwilei/O** 19

BRUNCH

Daniel Thiebaut | **Waimea/BI** 24
Hoku's | **Kahala/O** 26
Kozo Sushi | **Kahala/O** 20
Mariposa | **Ala Moana/O** 23
Z Orchids | **Waikiki/O** 26
Z Pahu i'a | **Kaupulehu-Kona/BI** 26
Plantation Hse. | **Kapalua/Ma** 25
Prince Ct. | **Waikiki/O** 22
Sam Choy's | **Iwilei/O** 19
Z Son'z | **Kaanapali/Ma** 24

BUSINESS DINING

Z Alan Wong's | **McCully/O** 28
Azure | **Waikiki/O** 25
Bali Steaks/Seafood | **Waikiki/O** 24
Beachhse. | **Waikiki/O** 23
NEW BLT Steak | **Waikiki/O** 24
Cafe O'Lei | **multi.** 24
NEW Cane & Taro | **Kaanapali/Ma** 19
Z Chef Mavro | **Moiliili/O** 27
David Paul's | **Lahaina/Ma** 26
Z Dondero's | **Poipu/K** 25
NEW Duke's Beach Hse. | **Kaanapali/Ma** 21
Gannon's | **Wailea/Ma** 23
Hoku's | **Kahala/O** 26
Hy's Steak | **Waikiki/O** 26
Indigo | **Chinatown/O** 21
Jimmy Buffett's | **Waikiki/O** 18
Z NEW Kauai Grill | **Princeville/K** 26
Kincaid's | **Ward/O** 20
Kobe/Oku's | **Waikiki/O** 22
Kona Inn | **Kailua-Kona/BI** 20
Z La Mer | **Waikiki/O** 28
Manta/Pavilion | **Kohala/BI** 25
Z Merriman's | **multi.** 26
Monettes | **Kohala/BI** 24
NEW Morimoto | **Waikiki/O** -
Morton's | **Ala Moana/O** 24
Z Nobu | **Waikiki/O** 27
Ola | **Kahuku/O** 21
Z Orchids | **Waikiki/O** 26
Red Salt | **Poipu/K** 26
Romano's | **Waikoloa/BI** 17
Z Roy's | **Hawaii Kai/O** 26
RumFire | **Waikiki/O** 20
Taormina | **Waikiki/O** 25
3660/Rise | **Kaimuki/O** 25
Verbano | **Waikiki/O** 19
Wolfgang's Steak | **Waikiki/O** 24

CELEBRITY CHEFS

Oliver Beckert
Z Lodge/Koele | **Koele/L** 27
Nicolas Chaize
Nico's/Pier 38 | **Iwilei/O** 25

Chai Chaowasaree
Chai's Is. | **Downtown/O** 25

Sam Choy
Sam Choy's | **Iwilei/O** 19

Fred DeAngelo
Ola | **Kahuku/O** 21

Mark Ellman
Mala | **Wailea/Ma** 25

John Ferguson
Kalaheo Café | **Kalaheo/K** 23

Hiroshi Fukui
Z Hiroshi | **Restaurant Row/O** 28

Beverly Gannon
Gannon's | **Wailea/Ma** 23
Z Hali'imaile Gen. | **Makawao/Ma** 27
Joe's B&G | **Wailea/Ma** 21

David Paul Johnson
David Paul's | **Lahaina/Ma** 26

Ed Kenney
Town | **Kaimuki/O** 24

D.K. Kodama
NEW Cane & Taro | **Kaanapali/Ma** 19
DK Steak House | **Waikiki/O** 22
Z Sansei | **Waikiki/O** 25
Vino | **Restaurant Row/O** 24

Seiya Masahara
Hakkei | **Makiki/O** 26

Nobu Matsuhisa
Z Nobu | **Waikiki/O** 27

George Mavrothalassitis
Z Chef Mavro | **Moiliili/O** 27

Peter Merriman
Z Merriman's | **multi.** 26

Jim Moffat
Bar Acuda | **Hanalei/K** 25

Masaharu Morimoto
NEW Morimoto | **Waikiki/O** -

Gerard Reversade
Z Gerard's | **Lahaina/Ma** 26

Roy Yamaguchi
Z Roy's | **multi.** 26

Laurent Tourondel
NEW BLT Steak | **Waikiki/O** 24

Alan Wong
Z Alan Wong's | **McCully/O** 28
Pineapple Rm. | **Ala Moana/O** 24

DINING ALONE

(Other than hotels and places with counter service)

Big City Diner | **multi.** 17
Blue Ginger | **Lanai City/L** 20
Bubba Burger | **multi.** 19
Burgers/Edge | **Kapahulu/O** 17
Cafe O'Lei | **multi.** 24
California Pizza | **multi.** 20
Downtown/HISAM | **Downtown/O** 24
Duane's Ono-Char | **Anahola/K** 24
Eggs 'n Things | **Waikiki/O** 22
Ezogiku | **multi.** 21
Fat Greek | **Kaimuki/O** 17
Genki Sushi | **multi.** 16
Goma Tei | **Ward/O** 22
Hale Vietnam | **Kaimuki/O** 22
Hanalei Gourmet | **Hanalei/K** 21
Hanapepe Café | **Hanapepe/K** 22
Helena's | **Kalihi/O** 25
Island Burger | **Ala Moana/O** 19
Kaka'ako | **Ward/O** 22
Koloa Fish | **Koloa/K** 24
Kona Brewing | **Hawaii Kai/O** 20
Kozo Sushi | **multi.** 20
Kua 'Aina | **multi.** 22
Mix Café | **Downtown/O** 21
NEW Monstera | **Kohala/BI** -
Nico's/Pier 38 | **Iwilei/O** 25

Olive Tree | **Kahala/O** 25
Ono Hawaii | **Kapahulu/O** 25
Panya | **multi.** 21
P.F. Chang's | **Waikiki/O** 19
Pineapple Rm. | **Ala Moana/O** 24
Shirokiya | **Ala Moana/O** 21
Side St. Inn | **Ala Moana/O** 24
Tangö | **Downtown/O** 24
Tanioka's | **Waipahu/O** 24
Taormina | **Waikiki/O** 25
Uncle's Fish | **Iwilei/O** 21
Verbano | **Aiea/O** 19

LOCAL FAVORITES

Aloha Mix Plate | **Lahaina/Ma** 21
Bamboo | **Hawi/BI** 23
Beach Tree | **Kaupulehu-Kona/BI** 24
Big City Diner | **multi.** 17
Blue Ginger | **Lanai City/L** 20
Brown's Bch. | **Kohala/BI** 24
Bull Shed | **Kapaa/K** 22
Buzz's | **Lanikai/O** 20
Café Pesto | **multi.** 23
Charley's | **Paia/Ma** 22
Downtown/HISAM | **Downtown/O** 24
Duane's Ono-Char | **Anahola/K** 24
Ezogiku | **Waikiki/O** 21
Flatbread | **Paia/Ma** 25
Fook Yuen | **McCully/O** 22
Genki Sushi | **multi.** 16
Goma Tei | **Ala Moana/O** 22
Green Door | **Chinatown/O** 22
Gyotaku | **multi.** 20
Z Hali'imaile Gen. | **Makawao/Ma** 27
Hanalei Dolphin | **Hanalei/K** 23
Helena's | **Kalihi/O** 25
Highway Inn | **Waipahu/O** 21
Huggos | **Kailua-Kona/BI** 21
Kaka'ako | **Ward/O** 22
Kanemitsu's | **Kaunakakai/Mo** 19
Kauai Pasta | **Kapaa/K** 22
Kenichi | **Keauhou/BI** 24
Kihei Caffe | **Kihei/Ma** 25
Kintaro | **Kapaa/K** 24
Koloa Fish | **Koloa/K** 24
Kona Inn | **Kailua-Kona/BI** 20
Kua 'Aina | **multi.** 22
Lighthouse | **Kilauea/K** 18
Little Village | **Chinatown/O** 23
Manago | **Captain Cook/BI** 21
Z Matsumoto's | **Haleiwa/O** 23
Z Merriman's | **multi.** 26
Ono Hawaii | **Kapahulu/O** 25
Pah Ke's | **Kaneohe/O** 22
Paia Fish Mkt. | **Paia/Ma** 26
Panya | **multi.** 21
Phuket Thai | **McCully/O** 23
Quinn's | **Kailua-Kona/BI** 21
RumFire | **Waikiki/O** 20
Sam Choy's | **Iwilei/O** 19
Side St. Inn | **Ala Moana/O** 24
Tangö | **Downtown/O** 24
Tanioka's | **Waipahu/O** 24
Tropical Taco | **Hanalei/K** 19
Yanagi | **Kakaako/O** 23

MEET FOR A DRINK

Z Beach Hse. | **Poipu/K** 24
NEW BLT Steak | **Waikiki/O** 24
Brasserie/Vin | **Chinatown/O** 22
Brennecke's | **Poipu/K** 19
NEW Cane & Taro | **Kaanapali/Ma** 19
David Paul's | **Lahaina/Ma** 26
DK Steak House | **Waikiki/O** 22
NEW Duke's Beach Hse. | **Kaanapali/Ma** 21
Duke's | **multi.** 20

Formaggio | **multi.** 21
Gannon's | **Wailea/Ma** 23
Hula Shores | **Kaunakakai/Mo** -
Indigo | **Chinatown/O** 21
Jimmy Buffett's | **Waikiki/O** 18
Joe's B&G | **Wailea/Ma** 21
Keoki's Paradise | **Poipu/K** 20
Kobe/Oku's | **Waikiki/O** 22
Kona Brewing | **Hawaii Kai/O** 20
Kona Inn | **Kailua-Kona/BI** 20
Lucy's Grill | **Kailua/O** 21
Manta/Pavilion | **Kohala/BI** 25
Monettes | **Kohala/BI** 24
NEW Monstera | **Kohala/BI** -
NEW Morimoto | **Waikiki/O** -
Z Nobu | **Waikiki/O** 27
Romano's | **Waikoloa/BI** 17
Z Roy's | **Hawaii Kai/O** 26
RumFire | **Waikiki/O** 20
Sarento's/Bch. | **Kihei/Ma** 25
Side St. Inn | **Ala Moana/O** 24
Stage | **Ala Moana/O** 22
Tiki's Grill | **Waikiki/O** 17
Town | **Kaimuki/O** 24
Umalu | **Kaanapali/Ma** 22
Vino | **Restaurant Row/O** 24
Wolfgang's Steak | **Waikiki/O** 24

NEWCOMERS

Beachhse. | **Waikiki/O** 23
Burgers/Edge | **Kapahulu/O** 17
Cane & Taro | **Kaanapali/Ma** 19
Downtown/HISAM | **Downtown/O** 24
Duo | **Wailea/Ma** 25
Fat Greek | **Kaimuki/O** 17
Flatbread | **Paia/Ma** 25
Hakkei | **Makiki/O** 26
Lanai City | **Lanai City/L** 23
MAC 24/7 | **Waikiki/O** 19
Z Nobu | **Waikiki/O** 27
Panya | **Ala Moana/O** 21
Stage | **Ala Moana/O** 22
Tangö | **Downtown/O** 24
Uncle's Fish | **Iwilei/O** 21
Waimea Brew | **Waimea/K** 17
Wild Ginger | **Kaimuki/O** 21

PEOPLE-WATCHING

Z Alan Wong's | **McCully/O** 28
Azure | **Waikiki/O** 25
Bar Acuda | **Hanalei/K** 25
NEW BLT Steak | **Waikiki/O** 24
Brasserie/Vin | **Chinatown/O** 22
Brennecke's | **Poipu/K** 19
Bubba Burger | **multi.** 19
Buzz's Wharf | **Maalaea/Ma** 20
Chai's Is. | **Downtown/O** 25
David Paul's | **Lahaina/Ma** 26
DK Steak House | **Waikiki/O** 22
Z Dondero's | **Poipu/K** 25
Duke's | **multi.** 20
Formaggio | **multi.** 21
Hoku's | **Kahala/O** 26
Indigo | **Chinatown/O** 21
Jimmy Buffett's | **Waikiki/O** 18
Keoki's Paradise | **Poipu/K** 20
Kincaid's | **Ward/O** 20
Z La Mer | **Waikiki/O** 28
Leilani's | **Kaanapali/Ma** 20
Manta/Pavilion | **Kohala/BI** 25
Mariposa | **Ala Moana/O** 23
Milagros | **Paia/Ma** 20
Monettes | **Kohala/BI** 24
NEW Morimoto | **Waikiki/O** -
Z Nobu | **Waikiki/O** 27
Z Orchids | **Waikiki/O** 26
Pineapple Rm. | **Ala Moana/O** 24

Z Roy's | **Hawaii Kai/O** 26
RumFire | **Waikiki/O** 20
Z Sansei | **multi.** 25
Side St. Inn | **Ala Moana/O** 24
Tiki's Grill | **Waikiki/O** 17
Town | **Kaimuki/O** 24
Umalu | **Kaanapali/Ma** 22

QUICK BITES

Antonio's | **multi.** 19
Big City Diner | **multi.** 17
Blue Ginger | **Lanai City/L** 20
Bubba Burger | **multi.** 19
Burgers/Edge | **Kapahulu/O** 17
California Pizza | **multi.** 20
Cheeseburger/Paradise | **multi.** 17
Downtown/HISAM | **Downtown/O** 24
Duane's Ono-Char | **Anahola/K** 24
Duke's | **multi.** 20
Eggs 'n Things | **Waikiki/O** 22
Ezogiku | **multi.** 21
Fat Greek | **Kaimuki/O** 17
Genki Sushi | **multi.** 16
Goma Tei | **Ward/O** 22
Hale Vietnam | **Kaimuki/O** 22
Hanapepe Café | **Hanapepe/K** 22
Helena's | **Kalihi/O** 25
Island Burger | **Ala Moana/O** 19
Jimmy Buffett's | **Waikiki/O** 18
Kaka'ako | **Ward/O** 22
Kalaheo Café | **Kalaheo/K** 23
Kanemitsu's | **Kaunakakai/Mo** 19
Kihei Caffe | **Kihei/Ma** 25
Koloa Fish | **Koloa/K** 24
Kua 'Aina | **multi.** 22
Mix Café | **Downtown/O** 21
Nico's/Pier 38 | **Iwilei/O** 25
Round Table | **multi.** 19
RumFire | **Waikiki/O** 20
Tanioka's | **Waipahu/O** 24
Tropical Taco | **Hanalei/K** 19
Umalu | **Kaanapali/Ma** 22
Uncle's Fish | **Iwilei/O** 21
Vietnam/Pho | **Chinatown/O** 25
Wahoo's Fish | **Ward/O** 18

QUIET CONVERSATION

Azure | **Waikiki/O** 25
Bali Steaks/Seafood | **Waikiki/O** 24
Beachhse. | **Waikiki/O** 23
Café Portofino | **Kalapaki Bch/K** 22
NEW Cane & Taro | **Kaanapali/Ma** 19
Z Chef Mavro | **Moiliili/O** 27
Z Dondero's | **Poipu/K** 25
NEW Duke's Beach Hse. | **Kaanapali/Ma** 21
Gannon's | **Wailea/Ma** 23
Hakkei | **Makiki/O** 26
Z NEW Kauai Grill | **Princeville/K** 26
Kauai Pasta | **Lihue/K** 22
Kona Inn | **Kailua-Kona/BI** 20
Z La Mer | **Waikiki/O** 28
Lighthouse | **Kilauea/K** 18
Z Lodge/Koele | **Koele/L** 27
Manta/Pavilion | **Kohala/BI** 25
Market Fresh | **Makawao/Ma** -
Z Merriman's | **multi.** 26
Monettes | **Kohala/BI** 24
Ola | **Kahuku/O** 21
Z Orchids | **Waikiki/O** 26
Romano's | **Waikoloa/BI** 17
Sarento's Top | **Waikiki/O** 19
Stage | **Ala Moana/O** 22
Tangö | **Downtown/O** 24
Taormina | **Waikiki/O** 25

ROMANTIC PLACES

Z Alan Wong's | **McCully/O** 28
Azure | **Waikiki/O** 25
Baci Bistro | **Kailua/O** 25
Bali Steaks/Seafood | **Waikiki/O** 24
Banyan Tree | **Kapalua/Ma** 24
Z Beach Hse. | **Poipu/K** 24
Beachhse. | **Waikiki/O** 23
Café Portofino | **Kalapaki Bch/K** 22
NEW Cane & Taro | **Kaanapali/Ma** 19
Casa di Amici | **Poipu/K** 23
Z Dondero's | **Poipu/K** 25
NEW Duke's Beach Hse. | **Kaanapali/Ma** 21
Gannon's | **Wailea/Ma** 23
Z Gerard's | **Lahaina/Ma** 26
Hau Tree | **Waikiki/O** 21
Hoku's | **Kahala/O** 26
Humuhumunukunukuapua'a | **Wailea/Ma** 22
Z NEW Kauai Grill | **Princeville/K** 26
Kimo's | **Lahaina/Ma** 21
Z La Mer | **Waikiki/O** 28
Lighthouse | **Kilauea/K** 18
Z Lodge/Koele | **Koele/L** 27
Manta/Pavilion | **Kohala/BI** 25
Z Michel's | **Waikiki/O** 27
Monettes | **Kohala/BI** 24
NEW Morimoto | **Waikiki/O** -
Nick's Fishmkt. | **Wailea/Ma** 23
Z Nobu | **Waikiki/O** 27
Ola | **Kahuku/O** 21
Z Orchids | **Waikiki/O** 26
Pacific'O | **Lahaina/Ma** 25
Plantation Gdns. | **Poipu/K** 23
RumFire | **Waikiki/O** 20
Sarento's/Bch. | **Kihei/Ma** 25
Sarento's Top | **Waikiki/O** 19
Z Son'z | **Kaanapali/Ma** 24
3660/Rise | **Kaimuki/O** 25
Z Tidepools | **Poipu/K** 24
Umalu | **Kaanapali/Ma** 22

SENIOR APPEAL

Assaggio | **Ala Moana/O** 21
Azure | **Waikiki/O** 25
Beachhse. | **Waikiki/O** 23
Big City Diner | **multi.** 17
Bull Shed | **Kapaa/K** 22
Buzz's | **Lanikai/O** 20
Café Portofino | **Kalapaki Bch/K** 22
Contemp. Café | **Makiki Hts/O** 21
Hanalei Dolphin | **Hanalei/K** 23
Hau Tree | **Waikiki/O** 21
Hy's Steak | **Waikiki/O** 26
Keoki's Paradise | **Poipu/K** 20
Keo's | **Waikiki/O** 22
Manta/Pavilion | **Kohala/BI** 25
Monettes | **Kohala/BI** 24
Ocean Hse. | **Waikiki/O** 24
Z Orchids | **Waikiki/O** 26
Original Pancake | **Kapalama/O** 21
Paesano | **Aiea/O** 20
Pagoda | **Ala Moana/O** 17
Pavilion Café | **Ala Moana/O** 24
Stage | **Ala Moana/O** 22
Taormina | **Waikiki/O** 25
Umalu | **Kaanapali/Ma** 22
Willows | **Moiliili/O** 18
Wolfgang's Steak | **Waikiki/O** 24

SPECIAL OCCASIONS

Z Alan Wong's | **McCully/O** 28
Azure | **Waikiki/O** 25
Bali Steaks/Seafood | **Waikiki/O** 24
Z Beach Hse. | **Poipu/K** 24
Beachhse. | **Waikiki/O** 23
NEW BLT Steak | **Waikiki/O** 24
Z Chef Mavro | **Moiliili/O** 27

David Paul's | **Lahaina/Ma** 26
Z Dondero's | **Poipu/K** 25
NEW Duke's Beach Hse. | **Kaanapali/Ma** 21
Gannon's | **Wailea/Ma** 23
Z Gerard's | **Lahaina/Ma** 26
Hau Tree | **Waikiki/O** 21
Hoku's | **Kahala/O** 26
Hy's Steak | **Waikiki/O** 26
Z NEW Kauai Grill | **Princeville/K** 26
Kobe/Oku's | **Waikiki/O** 22
Kona Inn | **Kailua-Kona/BI** 20
Z La Mer | **Waikiki/O** 28
Z Lodge/Koele | **Koele/L** 27
Manta/Pavilion | **Kohala/BI** 25
Mariposa | **Ala Moana/O** 23
Z Merriman's | **multi.** 26
Z Michel's | **Waikiki/O** 27
Monettes | **Kohala/BI** 24
NEW Morimoto | **Waikiki/O** -
Z Nobu | **Waikiki/O** 27
Ola | **Kahuku/O** 21
Z Orchids | **Waikiki/O** 26
Red Salt | **Poipu/K** 26
Z Roy's | **Hawaii Kai/O** 26
Sarento's Top | **Waikiki/O** 19
Stage | **Ala Moana/O** 22
3660/Rise | **Kaimuki/O** 25
Z Tidepools | **Poipu/K** 24
Wolfgang's Steak | **Waikiki/O** 24

TEEN APPEAL

Antonio's | **multi.** 19
Auntie Pasto | **multi.** 19
Benihana | **Waikiki/O** 19
Big City Diner | **multi.** 17
Brennecke's | **Poipu/K** 19
Bubba Burger | **multi.** 19
California Bch. | **Ward/O** 20
California Pizza | **multi.** 20
Cheeseburger/Paradise | **multi.** 17
Cheesecake Fac. | **Waikiki/O** 20
Duane's Ono-Char | **Anahola/K** 24
Duke's | **multi.** 20
Genki Sushi | **multi.** 16
Hard Rock | **Lahaina/Ma** 15
Hula Grill | **Waikiki/O** 21
Island Burger | **Ala Moana/O** 19
Kua 'Aina | **Ward/O** 22
MAC 24/7 | **Waikiki/O** 19
Z Matsumoto's | **Haleiwa/O** 23
Molokai Pizza | **Kaunakakai/Mo** -
P.F. Chang's | **Ala Moana/O** 19
Romano's | **Ala Moana/O** 17
Round Table | **multi.** 19
Sam Choy's | **Iwilei/O** 19
Shokudo | **Ala Moana/O** 22
Shore Bird | **Waikiki/O** 16
Tanaka | **multi.** 21
Tiki's Grill | **Waikiki/O** 17
Wahoo's Fish | **Ward/O** 18

TRENDY

Azure | **Waikiki/O** 25
Bar Acuda | **Hanalei/K** 25
NEW BLT Steak | **Waikiki/O** 24
Brasserie/Vin | **Chinatown/O** 22
David Paul's | **Lahaina/Ma** 26
Formaggio | **multi.** 21
Hanalei Gourmet | **Hanalei/K** 21
Z Hiroshi | **Restaurant Row/O** 28
Hoku's | **Kahala/O** 26
Ichiriki Nabe | **Ala Moana/O** 24
Manta/Pavilion | **Kohala/BI** 25
Monettes | **Kohala/BI** 24
NEW Morimoto | **Waikiki/O** -
Z Nobu | **Waikiki/O** 27
Ola | **Kahuku/O** 21

Red Salt | **Poipu/K** 26
RumFire | **Waikiki/O** 20
Shokudo | **Ala Moana/O** 22
Stage | **Ala Moana/O** 22
Tiki's Grill | **Waikiki/O** 17
Town | **Kaimuki/O** 24
12th Ave. | **Kaimuki/O** 24
Umalu | **Kaanapali/Ma** 22
Wolfgang's Steak | **Waikiki/O** 24

TWENTYSOMETHINGS

Azure | **Waikiki/O** 25
Bar Acuda | **Hanalei/K** 25
Brasserie/Vin | **Chinatown/O** 22
Brennecke's | **Poipu/K** 19
California Bch. | **Ward/O** 20
Casablanca | **Poipu/K** 18
Casa di Amici | **Poipu/K** 23
David Paul's | **Lahaina/Ma** 26
Duke's | **multi.** 20
Formaggio | **multi.** 21
Hanalei Gourmet | **Hanalei/K** 21
Hanapepe Café | **Hanapepe/K** 22
Hard Rock | **Lahaina/Ma** 15
Ichiriki Nabe | **Ala Moana/O** 24
Indigo | **Chinatown/O** 21
Jimmy Buffett's | **Waikiki/O** 18
Keoki's Paradise | **Poipu/K** 20
Little Village | **Chinatown/O** 23
Longhi's | **Ala Moana/O** 21
Lucy's Grill | **Kailua/O** 21
MAC 24/7 | **Waikiki/O** 19
Manta/Pavilion | **Kohala/BI** 25
Monettes | **Kohala/BI** 24
Z Nobu | **Waikiki/O** 27
Ola | **Kahuku/O** 21
Z Sansei | **Waikiki/O** 25
Shokudo | **Ala Moana/O** 22
Sorabol | **Ala Moana/O** 22
Tiki's Grill | **Waikiki/O** 17
Town | **Kaimuki/O** 24
12th Ave. | **Kaimuki/O** 24
Umalu | **Kaanapali/Ma** 22
Wolfgang's Steak | **Waikiki/O** 24

VISITORS ON EXPENSE ACCOUNT

Z Alan Wong's | **McCully/O** 28
Azure | **Waikiki/O** 25
Bali Steaks/Seafood | **Waikiki/O** 24
Banyan Tree | **Kapalua/Ma** 24
Z Beach Hse. | **Poipu/K** 24
NEW BLT Steak | **Waikiki/O** 24
Chai's Is. | **Downtown/O** 25
Z Chef Mavro | **Moiliili/O** 27
Ciao Mein | **Waikiki/O** 22
David Paul's | **Lahaina/Ma** 26
DK Steak House | **Waikiki/O** 22
Duo | **Wailea/Ma** 25
Ferraro's | **Wailea/Ma** 24
Z Gerard's | **Lahaina/Ma** 26
Hoku's | **Kahala/O** 26
Hulopo'e Ct. | **Manele/L** 23
Hy's Steak | **Waikiki/O** 26
Indigo | **Chinatown/O** 21
Lahaina Grill | **Lahaina/Ma** 26
Z La Mer | **Waikiki/O** 28
Z Lodge/Koele | **Koele/L** 27
Manta/Pavilion | **Kohala/BI** 25
Mariposa | **Ala Moana/O** 23
Z Merriman's | **multi.** 26
Z Michel's | **Waikiki/O** 27
Monettes | **Kohala/BI** 24
NEW Morimoto | **Waikiki/O** -
Ola | **Kahuku/O** 21
Z Orchids | **Waikiki/O** 26
Pineapple Rm. | **Ala Moana/O** 24
Red Salt | **Poipu/K** 26
Z Roy's | **Hawaii Kai/O** 26

SPECIAL FEATURES

Z Sansei | **Waikiki/O** 25
Z Son'z | **Kaanapali/Ma** 24
Z Spago | **Wailea/Ma** 26
Z Sushi Sasabune | **Ala Moana/O** 28
3660/Rise | **Kaimuki/O** 25
Umalu | **Kaanapali/Ma** 22
Wolfgang's Steak | **Waikiki/O** 24
Yanagi | **Kakaako/O** 23
Yohei | **Kapalama/O** 25

WINNING WINE LISTS

Z Alan Wong's | **McCully/O** 28
Azure | **Waikiki/O** 25
Bali Steaks/Seafood | **Waikiki/O** 24
Bar Acuda | **Hanalei/K** 25
Beachhse. | **Waikiki/O** 23
NEW BLT Steak | **Waikiki/O** 24
Brasserie/Vin | **Chinatown/O** 22
Café Portofino | **Kalapaki Bch/K** 22
Casablanca | **Poipu/K** 18
Casa di Amici | **Poipu/K** 23
Z Chef Mavro | **Moiliili/O** 27
DK Steak House | **Waikiki/O** 22
Z Dondero's | **Poipu/K** 25
Ferraro's | **Wailea/Ma** 24
Formaggio | **multi.** 21
Z Gerard's | **Lahaina/Ma** 26
Z Hiroshi | **Restaurant Row/O** 28
Hoku's | **Kahala/O** 26
Hy's Steak | **Waikiki/O** 26
Lahaina Grill | **Lahaina/Ma** 26
Z La Mer | **Waikiki/O** 28
Z Lodge/Koele | **Koele/L** 27
Manta/Pavilion | **Kohala/BI** 25
Z Michel's | **Waikiki/O** 27
Monettes | **Kohala/BI** 24
NEW Morimoto | **Waikiki/O** -
Nick's Fishmkt. | **Wailea/Ma** 23
Z Orchids | **Waikiki/O** 26
Pineapple Grill | **Kapalua/Ma** 25
Plantation Hse. | **Kapalua/Ma** 25
Z Roy's | **Hawaii Kai/O** 26
Z Son'z | **Kaanapali/Ma** 24
Z Spago | **Wailea/Ma** 26
Stage | **Ala Moana/O** 22
Z Tidepools | **Poipu/K** 24
Vino | **Restaurant Row/O** 24